Solo Acoustic Musician™

2

New Tips, Stories and SAM Interviews

Michael Nichols

Printed in the United States of America

ISBN: 978-1-956019-91-9 (paperback)
ISBN: 978-1-956019-92-6 (ebook)

Canoe Tree
Press

4697 Main Street
Manchester Center, VT 05255

Canoe Tree Press is a division of DartFrog Books.

TABLE OF CONTENTS

DEFINITION OF A SOLO ACOUSTIC MUSICIAN

Solo: Done by one person alone; unaccompanied.

Acoustic: Relating to sound or the sense of hearing. When referring to popular music or musical instruments: not employing electrical amplification.

Musician: A person who plays a musical instrument, especially as a profession, or is musically talented.

My definition of a Solo Acoustic Musician (SAM in the pages that follow) is straightforward: one person with an acoustic instrument, performing songs with or without vocals, hopefully for an audience.

There is something intrinsically pure about a person making music and singing songs with an acoustic instrument. To me, that's what a Solo Acoustic Musician is, and it's one of the most original and individual forms of musical expression.

A SOLO ACOUSTIC MUSICIAN'S CODE OF CONDUCT

Always be on time.

Dress appropriately for the gig.

Don't get drunk onstage or in the venue.

Clean up after yourself at the end of your gig.

Promote your music and your gigs.

Network with other musicians.

Use your gifts and talents to help others.

Show respect to yourself and others by not engaging in lewd language on the microphone.

Represent yourself, the agents, and the clients as best you can by being professional on the gig.

 # INTRODUCTION

The journey to my first book, *Solo Acoustic Musician: A Practical How-To Guide*, began precisely two years ago. Now, in May 2021, I offer SAM2, in which I will share new tips, stories, and even interviews with other Solo Acoustic Musicians.

I am happy to report that I have grown and learned more about being a SAM since the beginning of this process. As everyone reading this knows, many changes have occurred in the world, and the landscape faced by a working Solo Acoustic Musician became much more challenging. 2020 was an extraordinarily difficult year for anyone who makes their living playing gigs. As a SAM, I endured a feast-or-famine situation like nothing I'd ever encountered before. I am glad to say that the industry mobilized, coming together and supporting each other in unprecedented ways.

I have many Solo Acoustic Musician friends, and I thought I would ask some of them to tell a few of their favorite stories and expand on some of the ideas in the practical how-to guide. Every one of the SAMs I know does things a little differently. They may prefer different gear, use other techniques to work the crowd, and encounter different scenarios on gigs. In the pages that follow, I will share some of their stories from gigs that went well and ones that became train wrecks. We all love it when things go right, and a gig seems perfect. But here in the land of hindsight, I like to laugh at the random craziness that happens from time to time, and my friends have fun stories to share about when things go wrong. Through these interviews, I will also expand on other areas covered in the first book. My friends have different ideas about booking gigs, songwriting, and networking with other musicians. You will find out what they have to say in later chapters.

I have also interviewed a luthier from my area to share some expert advice about acoustic guitars. This guy is great at what he does, and I have trusted him to work on my Martin in the past. Tips about care and maintenance are essential things for a SAM to know. Our guitars are more than just a tool in the box, and we should take care of them as best as we can.

UPDATES: 2020 TO TODAY

In the last two years, I have adjusted my life in accordance with the ever-changing atmosphere of playing guitar and singing for a living. But there are many constants that probably won't ever change much for me.

I still show up on time for gigs, and I believe it's essential to do so. I maintain the same work ethic when it comes to this basic rule. I don't think it will ever change.

I have continued learning and arranging new songs to add to my songbook. One of the most fun things I can do, to keep things fresh for myself and my audience, has been to experiment with the work of new artists and "trying on" new styles of music. Trying to branch out stylistically has been really exciting. When I hear songs on the house stereo when I am setting up my equipment at gigs, when I'm walking through a store, or when I'm listening to the radio, I find myself writing down titles and making lists of new music to learn. Not every song I hear makes it to the performance stage, but I listen to each one on YouTube. I use the same process to learn and format songs for my songbook that I discussed in *Solo Acoustic Musician.*

All of us have favorite artists to cover, and there seem to be some traditionally famous artists everyone likes to cover. It is fun when we find an artist that is in both categories. Where I live, Tom Petty is always a good go-to artist to cover. I also enjoy his music, so it makes a great combination of being a desirable choice for the audience and for me. Playing one of his songs is almost always a hit and will receive applause. I have been playing several of his songs for many years. So, to keep things fresh for me, I recently learned a newer song of his, and I am having a lot of fun playing it. I would guesstimate that I currently have about eight to ten of his songs in my songbook, and there are still many more to learn.

I would like to offer something new as a suggestion, and a challenge for you: try to write at least one instrumental guitar song. If you can write more than one, you should go for it. While practicing or learning new things, I will come up with ideas and write new music on my guitar that does not have lyrics. I think some of these instrumental pieces sound cool, and I want to share them with the audience. As a Solo Acoustic Musician, I believe it's part of my job to showcase my guitar skills. Mixing in an instrumental adds to the musical landscape of my show. Over time, I have written quite a few instrumental ideas that I like to use on gigs. Sometimes I will use an instrumental that I have written as an introduction to a cover song that I play. It adds a creative dynamic to my set when I add one of these pieces to my show.

Recently I have started tracking how many new cover songs I have been learning. At the end of each week, I put the number of songs I learned that week in the margin on my calendar. I will add up a monthly total and do a yearly tally to see my progress. I will also add these numbers to my annual spreadsheet. I can add accountability to my mission of learning more songs by doing this.

Updating my gear and adding new items has been a part of reinventing myself over the course of my career. I have recently added new guitar pedals to my pedalboard that grant me increased looping abilities and help me to create a fuller sound. With the addition of an organ pedal and a keyboard pedal, I now can make my third loop layer very realistic. I use the organ pedal for a jazzy tone, and the keyboard pedal for a steel drum effect. The steel drum setting works for me because I live in a tropical vacation area in Florida, and I don't use it a lot, so it has a greater impact. When I am playing an acoustic guitar and suddenly it sounds like a steel drum, it turns heads.

I am still using the same guitar from my collection as my primary instrument, and have the same backup and knock-around guitars. I have not added a new guitar in a while. My choice for a new guitar has changed, but that is not the reason for the delay in buying a new one. Most of the major guitar manufacturers are behind schedule because of the shutdowns in 2020. So my timeline has been delayed, and I think I will be making a new guitar purchase later in 2022.

My main piece of P.A. gear is still my AER amp, but I will be trading in my Mackie speakers for updated models that include Bluetooth. Adding this feature to my speakers will eliminate a cable, making setup and breakdown that much quicker. By being able to go wireless, I will be able to use my phone or my iPad to play music during my breaks without needing an RCA cable. The RCA jack on the back of my amp has been used so much that it is damaged. I have bypassed that problem by adding a small $60 mixer to my backpack guitar case. It's a handheld-size five-channel Mackie Mix5, and it's the perfect tool for this situation. I have it set up to mute my cable with my tuner pedal. Then I unplug my guitar and plug my cable straight into the main out on the mixer. After that, I step on my tuner pedal again. Then my break music comes right from my iPad through the RCA cable into the mixer, which will send the music through my pedalboard.

I always have to take a second to make sure that any effect pedals are turned off. After all, it would sound funny to have a song playing through the delay pedal or any other effect pedal in the chain.

Updating my speakers to these newer versions will add positive features to my P.A. capabilities. And by doing this every few years, I will also benefit by still having trade-in value from my previous speakers.

Since my last book, I have been able to pay off my minivan, and it's incredible not to have payments right now. Maintenance is one more cost to add to our overhead as a SAM, and we need our vehicles to transport our equipment to gigs. I get my oil changes on time and make any repairs or updates that my mechanic suggests. Make sure you find a reliable, honest local mechanic and keep your vehicle in working order. Also, make sure you keep all receipts for everything involving your vehicle. You can use anything you do to your car on your tax returns. Every oil change, new tires, brakes, and any repairs you need to have done are part of your business expenses and can be written off at the end of the year.

My go-to gig snacks that I bring from home are still an apple or a banana. I have doubled down on my vigilance about trying not to eat French fries or processed, fried food on gigs. I still take advantage of any free food or monetary bar tabs as part of my pay, but I opt for something healthy. I usually get a big salad with protein, like chicken. But I am only human, and sometimes, I treat myself to an order of wings to take home at the end of a gig.

Resting my voice and drinking warm tea are still staples of my routine. In between gigs, resting my voice is important, and I enjoy my quiet time. I still carry Traditional Medicinal Throat Coat Tea in my guitar case. Quite often, I will ask the bartender for a cup of hot water and make myself a cup of tea. It always soothes my throat when I am in my first set and have just begun singing.

I have also added meditation to my health and nutrition routine. I have found some excellent podcasts for this on Spotify. I will relax on the beach during my off time and listen to Deepak Chopra, or shuffle through relaxing episodes hosted by other people. Sometimes I listen to these on my phone, plugged into my car, while driving to gigs. It calms me down in traffic and prepares me to walk into a busy restaurant or bar atmosphere. This technique can also be used mid-gig; I will go back to my car on a break and hear a pleasant, calming voice that puts me at ease. The sensory overload that busy places offer, coupled with the sometimes stressful situation of being on stage, can be overwhelming. By taking a short meditation break, I can find myself calm and ready for the next set after just a few minutes of peaceful breathing. I think it helps me focus on the task at hand and simplify the objective in my mind. The world is full of distractions, and sometimes I need a minute to focus and keep myself on track.

It's hard to admit this, but I have to be honest — I have not written any new songs in the last two years. While I have written new arrangements and loops for cover songs, I have not written any new original material in quite a while. I still feel fulfilled with my musical expression by being creative with how I am doing the latest cover songs that I add to my songbook. I hope to break out of my songwriting rut and write a new batch of original songs soon.

Over the last two years, I have found myself pleasantly surprised by the success of virtual tip cans. They seem to work for both online live streams and at in-person gigs. The addition of diverse ways listeners can tip has become an indispensable tool for any working SAM. I have a new merchandise table sign that helps people find me quickly on the apps. I place my "Tips" sign in front of me while I play, and people can see my app addresses from their tables. I have also found that people will stop by my merchandise table on their way out of the venue, take out their phones and take a picture of my "Tips" sign. A little later in the evening, after the gig, or even the next day, I will receive a virtual tip from someone who saw me play. When I receive the notification on my phone, I always smile because it's a surprise to get this tip. There is just a little added excitement to opening the app and saying thank you to the person. It seems like a convenient way for people to add money to my tip can on their own later. Some venues are even paying me now using Venmo and PayPal.

I have given my sign a fresh look by laminating it and placing it inside an acrylic frame, to protect it from the wind and the rain. I have used clear packing tape to cover and protect all the edges. I also use a small clamp to keep it from being knocked off the table. I am enjoying the look and the durability — it looks professional, and is built to last a long time.

Keeping connected with the network of local musicians has grown even more critical. I have to say I am proud to live where I do, and one big reason for that is the support of all the other local musicians. It feels like the musicians where I live have respect for each other and help each other when they can. I appreciate all the gig opportunities that come my way from other musicians. I am also grateful for the opportunity to be busy enough to reciprocate and send out gigs to my local friends.

When it comes to promotion, I have become more laid-back. With all the changes to the numbers of people allowed in venues and the distancing protocols, I don't feel it's essential to draw people to my shows, and I do my best to put on a good show for the ones who are there.

I can say one thing about booking, though. Old-school direct phone calls have been the best way to go lately. I still use email and send social media messages, but the phone calls that follow have been the most important. The same standards I talked about in my first book continue to apply. Stay persistent and follow up on your calls.

In *Solo Acoustic Musician: A Practical How-To Guide*, I discussed some of the techniques I use to book gigs. One meaningful change is a direct reversal of my previous strategy of booking a weekly weekend gig. What I mean by this is taking a gig at the same place every Friday or Saturday night. In the previous book, I recommended against this because it never was something that worked for me. In January of 2021, though, I was approached by a lovely little upscale restaurant that wanted to hire me to play every Saturday night. I was not interested at first, but then I decided to at least entertain the idea.

The main reason for my reversal was the wreck my calendar had been throughout the previous year. Finding some kind of stability is crucial for a working SAM. After thinking things through, I decided to negotiate the terms of the arrangement with the general manager and the head chef. I remembered that I had leverage because *they* had approached *me* with an offer. Because of this, I was able to add favorable terms to my deal with them. I was able to charge a little more money, get assurances of not being canceled for weather or other reasons, and get an agreement on a two-month notice period if they decided to stop or change from me playing every Saturday.

After the first two months of playing every Saturday night, I started to feel like part of the team. I remarked on this to the GM, and she replied, "That's because you *are* a part of our team!" Eventually, I learned that this restaurant had only lost three employees after five years of being in business. That meant everyone who worked there had been on the team a long time, becoming like a family. A high turnover rate for staff is a normal thing in this industry. The fact that this place did not have that problem was an excellent sign of stability. Now it is my job to keep the gig. As I discussed in the last book, one way to keep any weekly gig is to refresh the setlist to keep things fresh. So I have been adding new songs regularly and ensuring that I don't repeat the same older songs too many times. I have an extensive repertoire to pull from, and I like to mix it up. I hope to play for this establishment for a long time. I feel truly blessed to have lucked out and find myself a great, steady weekly gig.

Saying thank you for a gig to a venue owner, manager, or booking agent is more important now than ever. Everyone in our industry went through a horrible time with the shutdowns, and it's crucial to be grateful... and show that gratitude to those who hire you. Ensuring that your clients know that you appreciate them is vital in any form of sales, and booking gigs is a sales job, with you as both salesperson and product. I appreciate all the gigs that I book now more than ever. I smile when I get there, saying, "Thank you for the gig, I appreciate it, and I enjoy working with you."

My routines for loading in, setting up, breaking down, and loading out have not changed significantly, and I plan to stay consistent in these areas. Similarly, I have not made significant changes to my routines before, during, and after the gig. I keep things simple and efficient.

When it comes to working the crowd, I have added some jokes and stories that help me engage the audience. I am still a firm believer that if I can open up a dialogue with an audience, then I can have a better show. Some crowds are stiff, and others are more fun. It's always an adventure to find out which type is in front of me on any given night.

One night not long ago, I was dealing with a crowd that was not being responsive. After I had played five or six songs in a row to blank faces, I decided I needed to engage them somehow. So at the end of the next song, I said, "And the crowd goes wild!" This worked! At least half the crowd clapped and cheered. It is an old standby, and it can surprise a subdued audience into a response. But here is the catch: It won't work after every song. If I am going to use this line to engage the crowd, I must choose the right time to say it. If I do it at all, I will only do it once per show. It's like a magic trick, because you can't do it over and over, or its power will wear off.

In the previous book, I mentioned issues I've had when dealing with unexpected and unpredictable weather, and the period since has been par for the course. Rain, cold, heat, and humidity are constants where I live, and I have had cancellations due to harsh weather. On the other hand, I have been blessed with beautiful weather for many outdoor shows. It's always what it is, the weather.

In general, things still go wrong at more or less the same frequency as they always have, but they usually only happen one at a time. Adapting a problem-solving mindset and staying calm (remember what I said about meditation?) are still the best ways to respond to unpleasant surprises.

Since the release of *Solo Acoustic Musician*, I feel greater confidence when setting up and starting a gig. In chapter 16 of that book, Be A Pro, I discussed tracking. Keep track of your tips and learn from statistics. I want to add to this by suggesting that you keep a log or a "gig diary." It can be simple, with a date, time, venue, and detailed notes. Of course, you can also expand on any given gig with a more in-depth description of the events. Doing this could become an excellent tool to learn from your own work. You can look back at the good and bad gigs at the end of the month, year, or even a five-year period. You can analyze the information to find trends that can help you in your future booking pursuits. Maybe you can see a pattern of strengths and weaknesses where types of venues and situations are concerned. If you do better at private parties than in bars, for example, you can adapt your approach to choosing places and environments where you excel as a performer. You can also include data on song choices, setlists, and days of the week to adjust your show and perform better in places where a previous gig didn't go so well. A record like this can be a valuable resource.

After writing *Solo Acoustic Musician*, I found myself reflecting on my own words. I like to think I smile more often and do more of the positive, audience-affirming things I wrote about in that book. It's been a learning experience to hold myself to a standard that I wrote about and shared with others. I find it good to be personally accountable for what I say and do.

One thing I was on the fence about in *Solo Acoustic Musician* was writing about having a job part-time or full-time delivering pizza. I talked about moving somewhere new and establishing oneself in a completely new city. The subject matter and my personal experience were factual, so I left it in the book. I was 18 and 21 years old when I used this tactic to make money and learn my way around new cities after moving. During the last two years, I have watched the rise of Uber and DoorDash and other services like them, including delivery services from restaurants, increase tremendously. I know musicians who were able to support themselves through the shutdowns of 2020 by delivering food and groceries. In retrospect, I am glad I touched on taking that kind of job when needed. I am also delighted to see my working musician friends back to being full-time performers. It brings me immense joy to see their online posts about upcoming gigs!

MENTORSHIP: FINDING ONE AND BECOMING ONE

Mentor
— n. — an experienced and trusted adviser.
He was her friend and mentor until he died in 1915.
— v. — to advise or train (someone, especially a younger colleague).
...a site supervisor expertly mentored both trainees.

Mentorship
— n. — the guidance provided by a mentor, especially an experienced person in a company or educational institution.
His employees revered him for his mentorship and problem-solving qualities.
— n. — a period during which a person receives guidance from a mentor.
...a two-year mentorship with an entrepreneur in a tech start-up.

Is there a Solo Acoustic Musician in your area that you would like to talk to about being a SAM yourself? My advice is to go to one of their shows and ask them to talk after the set or when they're on a break. SAMs are traditionally more than willing to offer advice to someone who wants to be a working SAM. Although this is not always the case, I promise you that if you persist, you will soon find someone willing to help you with guidance at your beginning stages. This person could easily become a friend for life. Music has this way of uniting people and building friendships. Along the way, they can also become a valuable ally as you learn to navigate your local music scene.

Take your time in picking out someone to ask to be your mentor. You may need to talk to and ask different people if they would be willing to mentor you. This process is normal, and you should not get discouraged if it takes a little while to find someone who will spend their time with you.

Do I wish that I had a mentor when I started my musical journey? Or when I started playing guitar? Or when I started booking gigs? Of course I do, and had I had one, I probably would have avoided a few missteps along the way.

I did not have a singular individual who taught me what to do. Once I started gigging and becoming a regular at the local music stores, I began to gain a small amount of attention from the seasoned veteran musicians on the scene.

I started playing gigs when I was fourteen years old, and I was aggressive about my intention to get more and more. That meant that I was actively looking to buy and sell gear, in order to upgrade to better equipment. This led me to be in the store around other musicians and starting or joining conversations about places I had played. I also asked these other musicians about venues that I hadn't played yet.

I'm sure some of the older guys laughed at me or made jokes about my naïveté behind my back. Does that matter now? No, it does not. I never heard them laugh or poke fun at me when I was young, and even if I did, it wouldn't have mattered to me. I still would have continued my progression from my starting point to be able to create a life by playing music for a living. My goal, my aim, has always been to make a living playing live gigs.

As with any other challenge or goal in life, you must be careful who you listen to and who you let influence your thoughts. At the end of the day, you are responsible for the moves you make. You must believe in yourself and understand that your mentor can't do it for you.

As a collective, the other musicians around the stores were my mentors. I learned from them over time, and I appreciate the wisdom that I picked up here and there.

Your first mentor as a musician will usually arrive in the form of a teacher. The first instrument you learn about music on might not be a guitar. I started with the violin, and then I played saxophone. Neither of these lasted, and then I started playing guitar. I think all SAMs should get a guitar teacher in the beginning, and almost all of them will. This person could also be a schoolteacher for chorus, band, or drama. Whatever the case may be, your teacher will most likely be a mentor and influence your musical journey in the beginning. This mentor/protege relationship could last for a long time, too. Our teachers help us learn various aspects of being on stage and performing in front of an audience.

As a beginner Solo Acoustic Musician, I don't think it will be too difficult for you to find a mentor. I genuinely believe that you can get to know someone or even ask a local SAM for advice and to help you through mentorship. If that is not something you can achieve in person, I suggest you reach out on the internet to a person who plays music you enjoy. This method will require you to stand out in any way you can. To bridge the gap caused by being strangers, you will have to engage this potential mentor/teacher in a way that they feel their guidance and time will be appreciated and valued. Being on time for your meetings with a mentor is essential and shows respect.

Pro Tip: *Sometimes, a potential mentor will turn you down right away after your first request for their help. Please don't give up; try to convince them to be your mentor. Make a specific request for something you want to learn more about, and explain why you think they would be a great fit.*

You can become a mentor for someone else as well. As you grow your gig business and learn more about being a successful SAM, you can share your insights with others. One of our most basic needs as people in a social environment is to learn from others and teach those younger or less experienced than ourselves. This is true in many aspects of life.

There is no shortage of people who want to learn how to better themselves, so it won't be too hard to find someone with whom to share your ideas. Whatever your experience level or age, I am confident that you can learn from others while helping others learn from you. One of the best ways to understand your life lessons is to teach them to someone else. I don't suggest trying to "teach" someone else what to do when you are in the beginning or starting phase of your musical journey, but I do recommend that you develop friendships with people on your level and share things you learn with them. When I think back to when I was getting started, I wish I had more musicians my age to hang out with and share stories and tips with them. I didn't have anyone my age to bounce ideas off, because I started gigging when I was very young.

Becoming a mentor doesn't mean telling someone else what to do, or trying to control them. I think being a mentor means being available to offer advice and guidance about situations in the SAM path. I believe that for me, it means that I have to lead by example and try to be a positive role model for others. Offering emotional support and trying to help someone set goals for their career as a SAM are other things that I want to carry out.

Being there to listen to other SAMs when they have questions or concerns about what they need to get done is important to me. I like to make eye contact and let them know that I am listening with interest. I pay attention and try to offer objective ideas for either problem solving or growth. Every situation doesn't require a specific band-aid, and there are no one-size-fits-all solutions. There are many diverse types of people involved in the gig life, and every situation is likely to be different and need to be handled a little differently. I never want to act like I know it all, because I don't. Everyone has a different path in life, and this is particularly true for anyone who decides to be a Solo Acoustic Musician.

You can find a mentor, and you can be a mentor. I hope you do both in your career as a Solo Acoustic Musician.

THE MUSIC STORE AS MUSIC SCHOOL

When I was a teenager, I hung around the local music stores where I lived. We had three different stores in my town, each of them a small mom-and-pop place. I liked that I could become friends with the owners and the employees who worked for them. I always felt comfortable just stopping in to hang out. We didn't have any of the big corporate chain stores nearby.

Now and then, I would make a two-hour trip to the city to wander around in a couple of the warehouse-sized stores. I would also visit other small stores an hour away from home. But my main spots were the places right in my town. They were a big part of my musical growth and the evolution of my toolkit. I was gigging already, and I was full of energy, eager to learn more about the lifestyle. While in one of these stores, I would hear things about the life of a professional musician, and about developments in equipment. I know that the brands of guitars I played, and the types of songs I chose to learn, had to do with what I saw and heard in those stores.

Picking up knowledge about new gear is just as important now as it was back then. Recently, I was in my local store to learn more about the latest speakers available. It has been about four years since I updated my P.A. speakers, and I will be looking for replacements soon. The other day, I discussed the issue with a trusted employee at the store, and I think I have made my choice.

I don't like to hang out at the music store and noodle around on guitar. I decided long ago to come in with a purpose. I am not saying that I won't hang out in a music store and talk with other musicians or employees. If I want to wander around and check things out, I will. But I prefer to go to the store for one reason, and maximize the use of my time to accomplish that goal. I don't like to spend time trying out guitars, pedals, or any other instruments or gear unless I am looking to buy something.

Pro Tip: *Hide/stash guitar picks everywhere. Put them in your car, and put them inside the body of your acoustic guitar. Always keep some in your pocket. The coffee table, computer desk, and end table are all good places to leave a pick. Leave them everywhere!*

Developing friendships with people who work at your local music store is an important thing to do, and I encourage you to become familiar with the store employees and managers. They are most likely musicians, soundmen, or teachers actively involved in your music scene. They do what they do for the commissions they earn per sale, of course, but they will also let you know about upcoming sales and promotions in the store, and about things going on in the wider world of local music. Networking with them could lead to gigs, a duo partner, bandmates, and saving money on gear through updated sale information. You might also find a mentor or guitar teacher in the form of a knowledgeable music store employee.

I always try to support my local music shop. Even if I want to order something they don't have in stock, it will help them stay in business and keep the doors open by ordering the items through them and picking them up from the store when they arrive. Every time that I go to one of my stores, I buy something. Even if I go looking for something specific and don't find what I want, I will buy a pack of strings or other accessories that I might need. I might grab a couple of stickers. Anything that I can do to give back to my local store. The music store and I are a part of the same music community.

I have been in music stores across the country, and I always try to establish some sense of rapport, even if I am just traveling through that town and don't know if I will ever be back to that store. You never know when you may see that person again or find yourself walking into that store again. It's always good to make friends in every music store you visit, so that in the future, you might walk through the door to a familiar face who also remembers you.

This doesn't mean that every place is equally great. Some music stores that I have been to in the past weren't much more than pawnshops. My sincere suggestion is to frequent or use honest or professional music stores. It doesn't have to be a big chain store to achieve this objective. I have been to small shops that were super professional and had excellent customer service. Furthermore, I think that the smaller shops seem to appreciate my business a little more than the big box stores. So I try to give them my money first if I can.

Your local music store is one of the first places you should look for a guitar teacher. Of course, you can also find teachers online now, on websites like TrueFire, or through a music school like the School Of Rock, which has many franchise locations.

If you are lucky enough to have a family member or friend who plays guitar, maybe they can be your first teacher and help you learn the basics. There are some people in this world who will not have a teacher at all, and who will learn the guitar all on their own by ear and feel. As a Solo Acoustic Musician, I suggest you find a guitar teacher, though, in the hope of bypassing years of trial and error as you learn your instrument.

While many resources for learning to play guitar are available online, and I know it's possible to pick up skills this way, I also believe that a one-on-one firsthand approach with a teacher is the best way to learn the instrument. You will probably have several guitar teachers as you grow and learn. When the one-on-one approach is supplemented by online resources, it will offer a powerful combination for learning.

Pro Tip: *What you practice relentlessly will be what you find yourself doing during a live show. You will probably not make up new licks live on stage. Pro players are responsible for every note they will play for an audience, and they know what they will play in advance. The more you practice, the more you will be prepared for what you can do on a gig.*

Whether you want to take guitar lessons, voice lessons, or music theory classes, you must be willing to be a student. It doesn't matter what age or skill level you have achieved. If you desire to learn and become better at your craft, you can make improvements.

Being a good student goes beyond being on time for your lessons, making sure you practice, and following your teacher's directions. You will be learning about music theory, chord progressions, scales, and finger positions. The technical aspects of music can seem monotonous and challenging to understand. This concept can be true when learning the finer points of anything. So along the way, don't be afraid to ask questions about specific things you want to know. Take an active role in your learning process. If there is a style of music or a particular song that you want to learn, ask your teacher to help you. This inquiry can be a massive advantage for getting where you want to be in your musical journey. The person teaching may not know what you want to achieve in music. Expressing your interests to them will make it easier for your teacher to create lessons specifically for you and guide you on your path.

One way to lose a teacher is for them to constantly teach you the same things over and over with no progress — because you're not practicing, and not actually trying to get better. Good teachers can tell when you haven't done your homework. It doesn't matter if you are paying them for their time. If they are a good teacher and you are not following their directions, they may lose interest in you as their student. Once you've made the effort to find a good guitar teacher, you must follow through and try to learn. Studying the lessons and practicing are necessary to build your skills on the guitar. You do not want to be dropped as a student and you do not want to waste your money, time, or the teacher's time. Teachers will graciously release you from their student roster if you do not prove yourself by improving your skills after their instructions.

Over time, what you want to learn will change, and you can always address your desires as you grow. If you want to learn blues, then ask. If you want to learn fingerstyle guitar techniques, then ask. If you don't know what you want to learn technically or stylistically, you can share your desire to learn specific songs with them. The songs that you want to learn will be full of the things they need to teach you, and yes, you can be this direct. Even your teachers need direction. If you can tell them what you want to learn, you can speed up your learning process and achieve your goals sooner.

As I mentioned before, I think that every guitar teacher will want to show you chords, scales, and basic guitar theory. So, if that is a given, just imagine how much farther you can advance if you also add what you want to learn to the mix. As you realize that all the technical stuff will also be in the songs you want to learn, it will make it easier to tackle your practice routines. All the hard work will make sense after seeing the improvements in your playing and having fun playing the songs you want to play. The results of adding direction to your lessons will be quickly noticeable.

I know it can be hard to ask about what kind of music you want to play. As you grow musically, your desire to learn assorted styles of music may change. I have known teachers that are fluent in all styles of music — they know music theory and can adapt this knowledge to their students' wants and needs. If you feel stagnant with a teacher, you can always move on to another person who may better fit who you are now. You have to continue to chase the musician you want to become. You must explore every available possibility to learn and master your instrument.

If you're a musician, it means you're going to die
unfulfilled... you'll spend the rest of your life on
an upward learning curve because you'll never be
as good as you can be. You'll die an apprentice, a
student, and there's nothing better than that. To have
achieved the best you can ever be — that's a tragedy.
—Pete Seeger.

I have played the guitar for a long time, and I certainly do not know it all. I find myself in periods of learning and periods of execution. I learn things, and then I apply them to real-life situations while I am playing songs. One part is learning and practicing a technique, and the other part is the expression and application of the technique in a song during a live performance.

The meaning of life is to find your gift.
The purpose of life is to give it away.
— Pablo Picasso

There are two primary components of being a Solo Acoustic Musician. Playing guitar is the first and most important, but you can also add singing. Instrumental acoustic guitarists are SAMs, but most working SAMs are singers as well and use both skills to present their material to an audience during a performance. This chapter includes my perspectives about both. I played guitar and sang for a long time, and I didn't address these two individually in my first book. I didn't even discuss them as dual skills together. SAM1 was not meant to teach you to play guitar or sing, and neither is SAM2. I hope that the information in this chapter will either show you or remind you of essential strategies to improve your skills as a Solo Acoustic Musician.

I have listed and described some of my favorite musical terms as they apply to singing. Most of us SAMs don't have formal training backing up our vocals, but we have a natural ability to sing. I believe these words can be learned and used to add more to our overall skill set. When I learned about dynamics and mic control, I was able to gain ground and reach another level with my singing abilities. Later in life, I was also able to talk about and share this information with other singers I met along the way — and now I'm passing it on to you.

 **SINGING**

I was blessed to have grown up singing in church and school. My mother was a music teacher and a church organist, and the choir director for both church and school. I had other teachers at church and school when I was growing up, too, but my family would sing together around the piano at home. I learned basic singing knowledge and techniques at an early age. I sang in group settings and even by myself at home, or if I was chosen for a solo performance. I learned the technical stuff that you can learn from music and chorus teachers.

I am not here to teach you about those things. There are books, videos, websites, and yes, professional vocal coaches. There are also institutions where you can learn about singing, like a school or a church. Usually, one of those places will have a teacher or choral director who can and will help you learn and improve. I didn't address singing in my first book because it is not an instruction manual on how to sing. In the pages that follow, though, I will share ideas or philosophies that I have developed over my years of singing. These thoughts will also apply to being a Solo Acoustic Musician.

I have been playing guitar and singing for a long time now. I sing both on and off microphone. Between learning and practicing songs and then playing them live through the P.A. at gigs, I have spent most of my life singing. I like to sing along to songs I hear on the radio. Yes, when I am driving in the car or even walking through the grocery store, I might be singing along to the songs on the radio or in-store music system. I know you probably do the same thing.

When I am learning a song, I do not sing at full volume, and I will stay in my lower register. Usually, when I am learning a song, I work out the guitar and vocal parts simultaneously. I might isolate the guitar part for a bit, but I am also thinking about what the words are, the melody, and how I am going to be singing the words onstage. Eventually, I will be playing the guitar part and start to incorporate the vocal layer on top and explore where I want to go with it and seeing what feels comfortable. I do not strain to hit notes that I can't.

I try to find out if the song is in a key I want to sing in, or if I think I can sing it firmly. Can I perform it well? Can I perform it very well? There is an enormous difference. Can I sing this song *and* sell it when I add the guitar part? I think about all these questions as I first attempt a song. When I am singing it into the microphone, it will change everything, and either be excellent or not what I want. The good news is that there are so many songs to try that I can always drop a song from my book if I don't like it. It's not the end of the world to decide to get rid of a song. More songs are written every day, and I only do myself a favor by sticking with songs that I think I perform very well. I love it when I find a song that I can play and sing at an elevated level. It is an incredible rush when it happens. Not every song does that for me.

MIC CONTROL

Mic control is another way of expressing what the rapper KRS-One calls "breath control": a performer's ability to breathe in between words and verses to make it sound as if they are not pausing to take breaths. It's a combination of using words that allow you to inhale and exhale, and masking your breaths with pauses that don't sound artificial. This skill is crucial when you have a mic up to your mouth, which will broadcast the sound of breathing just the same as it will broadcast your words.

Singers can control the volume of their voice during live performances, not only with their vocal cords but also with the microphone. By pulling the mic away from the mouth or bringing it closer, a vocalist can adjust and compensate depending on the characteristics of their voice or the lyric being sung, the microphone itself, and the venue's acoustics. This technique is often necessary when there aren't dedicated sound engineers monitoring the mix to adjust the levels or when dynamic compression isn't available to automatically adjust them on the fly.

As a Solo Acoustic Musician, I do not hold the microphone in my hand. When I want to exercise mic control, it usually means that I physically move my head away from the microphone. Sometimes I shift to the side, or back away from the microphone. The most drastic adjustment would be to turn my head, or to look up and sing a big note. This last one usually happens when I am in a small room with excellent acoustics, and I probably don't even need the mic for the big notes.

It is all about feeling. Try different things to learn how you sound on your microphone. You can put your mouth right on the microphone, touching it, or you can try to stay positioned within one to three inches away. There are different schools of thought on this, so you will find different directions or advice if you search for information on YouTube. Once again, I suggest that you see what feels good or sounds good to you personally when you try things out. The most important thing about mic control is that you can physically use your body to control your volume.

DYNAMICS

The varying volume levels in distinct parts of a musical performance are dynamics.

As a SAM, I must control how softly or loudly I sing into the microphone. Dynamics is the word that describes this technique. I can whisper or scream the notes that I am singing, and I can make my voice louder or softer based on my desire to affect the mood of a song. A song can start softly and get louder as it continues until it reaches a climax in volume, only to settle back down into a quiet ending. Think of the Radiohead song "Creep," where the verses are quiet, almost a murmur, but the chorus is sung at full voice (and accompanied by heavy guitar). This volume change would be an example of dynamics. It is an essential part of musical expression, and it is also one of my favorite terms when it comes to talking about music.

PRONUNCIATION

Pronunciation is how you say a word. An example of pronunciation is the difference in how people say the word tomato ("to-may-to" versus "to-mah-to") and how the words of a language are made to sound when speaking. Example: "His Italian pronunciation is terrible."

When I am singing, I want to put out the lyrics or words so that people can understand what I am saying, but I can change the way I pronounce a word to fit the song. If we used the example above of the word tomato, let's pretend we could change the pronunciation based on a rhyme scheme. (Tomato like "potato" or tomato like "roboto".) In other words, we would choose to pronounce "tomato" based on another word we were trying to rhyme it with in the lyrics.

DICTION

The style of enunciation in speaking or singing. "Enunciate" means to articulate and pronounce all the syllables of words.

As a SAM, diction is part of singing clearly — you want the audience to be able to clearly make out what the lyrics are and hopefully understand the overall message of the song.

INFLECTION

Inflection is the modification of a word to express grammatical information.

Inflection most often refers to pitch and tonal patterns in a person's speech: where the voice rises and falls. (Pitch and tone are not volume changes.) But inflection also describes a departure from a standard or straight course. When you change or bend the course of a soccer ball by bouncing it off another person, that's an example of inflection.

Inflection, or voice modulation, is a change in the pitch or tone of the voice. It's also sometimes referred to as "vocal melody," and every language and every regional dialect has its own vocal melody. Think about what a person sounds like speaking French, versus what a person sounds like speaking German. Think of what someone from New York sounds like when they talk, versus what someone from Georgia sounds like. These are examples of intonation, or vocal melody. Varying your tone throughout a speech – raising your voice slightly to indicate a question, lowering it to end a declarative sentence, speaking louder to show excitement or softer to express sadness – will help keep your audience interested.

Inflection allows you to emphasize keywords and emotions and helps convey your exact meaning to the audience. If you take the word "Hey" and say it several different ways, it can mean different things, or even mean the same thing in a different context. Maybe you bump into a friend who just got dumped, and when you say hi, they respond with a low soft tone and say "hey" in a sad voice. Or maybe you are trying to hail a cab, and you shout "hey!" very loudly as a taxi goes by you.

Here are five different ways the same combination of words can carry different meanings:

YOUR guitar is too loud.

Your GUITAR is too loud.

Your guitar IS too loud.

Your guitar is TOO loud.

Your guitar is too LOUD.

PASSION + EXPRESSION = ARTICULATION

Passion: strong and barely controllable emotion.

Expression: The process of making one's thoughts or feelings known.

Articulation: Using emotion to express an idea or feeling fluently and coherently.

In music, you can use your emotions to let everyone know how you feel in an obvious way. Are you happy? Are you sad? Are you angry? Are you in love? If you are enthusiastic about a song, you can tap into the emotion that it makes you feel. That's when you can express your feelings for everyone to hear.

If you articulate your message through your instrument, your voice, and your choice of words at the same time, then you might be able to evoke these feelings in others in the audience. Have you ever felt something when you heard a person perform a song? Have you ever wanted to cry or laugh while listening to a piece of music? Were they passionate? Were they using their voice to sing a lyric with an almost uncontrollable sadness? Did they close their eyes or seem to lose themselves in the music?

Maybe they transferred a feeling onto you through their passion and expression. It could've been on a CD or a TV or live in person. Do you think you can evoke a feeling in someone else when you sing a song?

MORE ABOUT BREATHING

When I was in chorus and choir as a kid, I learned about breathing when singing. For a SAM, my advice is to think consciously about when you need to take a breath. You may have been singing and playing for a while and not know what I mean because it comes naturally. I am trying to point out that when you are working on a song with lyrics that go fast, or there is a big note that you must hold for a long time, you will have to find a good spot in the song to take a big strategic breath. It is another part of the pattern of playing the song, just like when you plan to move your hand from one chord to another. Do you have a song where you switch from one chord to another, and the chords are far apart on the guitar neck? You probably have to look down and move your hand very fast from one spot on the neck to the other if you do. I am sure you know that the chord change is coming, and you are mentally preparing to make the change. You probably worked on it when you were practicing and learning the song. Planning when you need a big breath is the same thing, and is part of working up music for your performances.

Learning how to do it right can take your songs and performance to another level of professionalism. Most audience members won't notice that you did it, but you will know. On the other hand, if you don't do it and run out of breath, everyone will know. This skill is good to put some effort into, and will pay off during your show.

EMULATION

Emulation is the attempt to match or surpass a person or achievement, typically by imitation. In the context of musical performance, it refers to trying to sing and sound like someone other than yourself. Most likely, the person who sings the song that you are learning. Imitating someone can be fun, and the audience may respond to what you are doing.

Do you ever hear a song and try to sing like the person singing the song? I have done it many times in the past. I don't think I can ever sing precisely like someone else, but it is fun to try.

Have you ever been playing a gig and had someone walk up to you and say, "You sound like so-and-so"? Or "You should learn so-and-so's songs because you sound just like them"? Have you ever tried to sound like the person who wrote and sings the music you are learning? I have expressly tried to emulate other people's voices in the past. There are times when I feel like I can get into the other singer's voice and perform a good version of the song.

I feel like I can change my voice in a lot of ways. I can sing in a "blues voice," a "country voice," a happy or sad voice, and more. I have a "radio DJ voice" I can use. When I make announcements, I will use a particular voice. I can also emulate specific people well. I have had people tell me they think I sound like some very popular singers, including Cat Stevens, Dave Matthews, Eddie Vedder, John Mayer, Adam Sandler, Ed Kowalczyk, Johnny Cash, Neil Young, Bruce Springsteen, Chris Cornell, Tom Petty, and more. I don't even sing songs by some people on this list, but people tell me that I sound like them.

I have tried to sound like people over the years and have attempted to sing like them when I covered one of their songs. I used to ride along in my car and try to sing like the artist I was listening to, and I would put in a CD and play a song repeatedly. Now I stream the music or artist on my phone through the Spotify app. It can be a great learning tool. I learned how moving my mouth into certain positions or changing how I open my mouth can change how my voice sounds. I am saying that to sound like someone and sing like someone requires learning how to sing like them, which is the physical part of making me sound like them.

I don't know if I sound like any of these people, but when I am covering one of their songs, I can try and emulate more than just the tone. I can try to capture the feel or the vibe of a song and add it to my performance. It can give a song something extra that will make the crowd respond. There are a lot of individual things that people do when they sing. The way they pronounce a word, for example, could be significant to a specific song. It can be just that tiny of a thing that makes a song uniquely presented. When trying to sound like someone else, you might want to try to do something different with your body. Maybe you move your mouth differently. You can move your tongue or lips into various shapes, affecting your tone of voice when you sing. It has a lot to do with feeling. When you cover a song, you can feel like the original version as you perform it. It can be significant for your performance in a live setting. In a way, you are recreating the song or performance of someone else. You can also make it your own and create your version, but it starts with an interpretation of the original song you are covering. Cover songs are never just a copy because we are always putting a little of our own soul into the performance.

Two other words that I like which are related to emulation are mimic and impression.

A mimic is a person who copies the behavior or speech of other people. An impressionist is a performer whose act consists of imitating celebrities' and cartoon characters' sounds, voices, and mannerisms. Usually, the most impressive aspect of the performance is the degree of vocal fidelity to the target, usually a politician or a famous person.

HARMONY

As a Solo Acoustic Musician, I don't get to sing harmony parts very often, but I think it is a valuable skill to have.

Practicing harmony vocal lines is part of being a better musician. I know many people like me who perform by themselves, and now and then, I get the chance to see one of them play. Sometimes they will ask me to sing a song with them. I am always singing the lead lines of songs because I am the only one singing when I perform. So, when I have a chance to get up and sing along with a friend, it is fantastic to try and go for a harmony line. I used to do harmony parts a lot when I was young. Singing in church and school was always a chorus or choir group atmosphere that required singing distinct parts. I will admit that I am out of practice, and I could use refresher sessions for my skills to improve.

There are many Solo Acoustic Musicians who are now using technology to provide harmony lines to their live shows with the use of a harmony foot pedal. I have no experience using any of these pedals, but I have seen and heard others use them on gigs. It might be something that you can add to your toolbox and enhance your live show.

Having the ability to sing harmony parts can also help you in your songwriting. Creating layers of notes makes chords and that is a great way to express harmony lines. That leads me to think about creating layers of guitar parts with my looper. So, let's talk about guitar playing for a little bit.

# PLAYING GUITAR

There are similarities between singing and playing guitar, at least where live performance is concerned. In both cases, trying to sound like someone else is a terrific way to begin learning music and songs. Reaching a point where you can create your sound and music is more of a long-term goal. By studying every possible thing I can find or am interested in, I can start to find my own way of making music.

I have no intention of teaching you how to play guitar, although I can pass on some general ideas to you. You are going to learn chords, scales, etc. You can use all this information or theory to play all the assorted styles and genres of music. It would be best to embrace working on specific sounds and figuring them out from the inside: a blues song, a country song, a reggae song, a rock song. You should work on any other type of song that you hear, too. You never know what kinds of songs you might be good at or like to play, and you might surprise yourself.

You should also try both major approaches to guitar: playing with a pick and without. I know fantastic flatpickers who always play with a pick, and I know other players who prefer never to use one. It's a personal choice. The sounds and techniques you'll achieve either way are vastly different. I have always used a flat pick and never learned the finger-picking style, though I have written a few songs with basic fingerpicking techniques. I am always learning, so maybe I will spend more time with my fingers and take my skills up a notch. Time will tell.

They say that ten thousand hours of practice are required to achieve mastery. I would suggest that you try everything you can on your guitar. During those hours, learn as many skills as possible. Seek out new knowledge and try to have fun along the way. So many metaphors and analogies come to mind. You can pretend it's a video game and try to advance and unlock new levels. You could create a mission-style objective list like this:

- Learn a new chord progression

- Learn to solo over that chord progression

- Learn to write a song

- Learn a new trick on your guitar

- Learn a new rhythm style on your guitar

- Learn a new scale on your guitar

- Learn a fingerpicking technique

- Learn a new picking technique

- Learn a new chord

- Learn a music theory term and its definition, and apply it to a song (example: dynamics)

As you progress, you can make new lists with new goals. You can keep them in a folder or on a spreadsheet, and track changes as you go. It is one way to make yourself accountable for your growth.

You do not have to do these things in any specific order, but they can give you ideas of places to start with or go to, especially when you are stagnant. You can use your mission list to jump-start your practicing and get you out of a rut. Just look at your list and randomly pick a goal. Now you are on a mission.

Learn as many licks and tricks as you can. Do something that sounds cool. Sometimes when I do a pick slide on the acoustic guitar, it will catch somebody's ear in the audience and grab their attention.

Here is a tip for you when you are using a loop pedal: Before you start the loop, turn your guitar volume down ¼ to ½ the volume. After you have built your loop and added any other layers on top of it, turn up your guitar to full volume to play lead lines over the loop. Also, when setting your loop, you can use a palm mute to lower the volume or distinguish a part from the other parts. The best example of this is when you create a bass line and want it to have a controlled tone.

When playing lead over a loop, you can use your foot to turn on a delay pedal, put your fret hand over the sound hole, and press down on the strings. When you play these notes, it will be a percussive sound. The added delay will turn some heads because it's not a traditional sound people hear from an acoustic guitar. Think of Tom Morello of Rage Against the Machine, and how he creates sounds with his guitar. You can do the same things with an acoustic and the addition of effects pedals.

Did you know that you can talk into your guitar because most acoustic-electric models have a microphone inside them? There is a balance between the input jack and the microphone positioned inside the guitar's body. Try it. Plug the guitar into the P.A., turn the volume up, put the sound hole up in front of your face, get close, and talk or sing into your guitar. Now do it again with an effect like a delay pedal and see what things you can do with this combination of non-traditional techniques.

As a musician, I have learned by listening to and trying to sound like other people. Playing guitar or singing like another person is part of learning and finding out what I am good at covering musically. Hopefully, over time, I can find my way to develop my complete sound. I hope you explore music to find what you like and are good at doing. If you listen to and try to play assorted styles and genres of music, you will expose yourself to many rhythms and melodies. These differences in your listening journey will influence your performances and songwriting.

Pro Tip: *Have you ever seen someone using a beer bottle to play slide guitar? I don't suggest doing this with your acoustic guitar. Maybe doing something like it in the rowdiest dive bar will be fantastic. It's just a gimmick, though, and even if you do it correctly, I don't think it's appropriate to do this on most gigs. In general, it is more of an electric guitar player's move, so be careful with your acoustic guitar.*

METRONOMES

A metronome is a device used by musicians that marks time at a selected rate by emitting a regular tick. You can buy a metronome at your local music store or order one online. A tuner/metronome combo is a rather common find. And yes, you should buy one and learn how to use it. I will add that as I explained in my first book, you should buy two. Who knows, maybe even three.

I used to keep one in my vehicle so that I could count as I drove to a gig. If you don't have a metronome to keep in your car, you can count time to the songs on the radio or whatever you listen to music on while driving to a gig. You can also watch online videos or ask your teacher or a friend to teach you how to use a metronome. Even if you are an experienced guitar player, I suggest that you get yours out of storage, dust it off, and practice with it again, because you already know how valuable it is to work with one. This device will help you with your timing in your playing. You want to play your guitar in time, and you want to sing on key.

Learning to play your rhythms and keep a steady beat or groove is very important as a Solo Acoustic Musician, because you are the only instrument. There is no drum set, so you are it for the song's rhythm.

You can double or triple down on this concept if you want to make a loop pedal an addition to your show, because you are now becoming multiple tracks that need to layer together on time. By adding a bass line or a percussive knock on the guitar body, you add to the groove beyond just the rhythm guitar part. By looping this, you are creating a musical landscape. It is essential that the beginning and end of your loop are seamlessly smooth, but the timing of your other layered parts needs to be in time as well.

Practicing with other musical sources — CDs, or streaming audio or video — is a way to work on your time with an alternative metronome. Sometimes I play along on my guitar while sitting on the couch and watching a movie. The music changes keys and rhythms throughout the film, so I get exposed to assorted styles. I can pull up YouTube on my phone, my iPad, my computer, or my TV, and search for any kind of instrumental music. This type of practice is a terrific way to explore sounds. I can try to figure out the chords or the root notes, I can try to find the melody or the horn line, I can try to play a scale and create a lead line over the music, or I can see that there may be an infinite number of ways that I can use this tool for expression and learning music.

I didn't have access to this technology when I grew up in the Eighties. I had to play along with the radio or a cassette. I would try to learn the chord chart, try to play the melody of the lyrics, and try to feel the rhythmic value of the song.

Music surrounds us and is a significant part of our everyday lives, so we almost always hear or feel rhythms and melodies. These musical ideas ultimately affect our own music, and in this case, we are talking about time and the secret metronome that is always there. The next time you listen to the radio, I want you to start counting:

1, 2, 3, 4
1 &, 2 &, 3 &, 4 &
1-e & a, 2-e & a, 3-e & a, 4-e & a...

I was counting the rhythms I heard on the radio when I was driving my van to a gig. A song called "Feel Good Inc." by the band Gorillaz came on. As I counted and the song progressed, it came to a moment where all the drum parts disappeared. I kept counting, and when the drum parts came back in, I was right on time with them. It stuck out in my mind as a fitting example of counting along with a song on the radio. It is also a great reminder that as a Solo Acoustic Musician, I do not have a drummer with me, and I still have to count.

The aim is to count or even clap your hands on time to any and every song by being able to measure the most basic four-count of 4/4 music. It may seem basic to some and new to others, but I will tell you this: it doesn't matter what level of music you are currently experiencing or expressing. This type of practice is what the top people do. They count. They understand the count and its importance to the language.

I learned a lot on my own, and I don't have formal music theory school training. Let me tell you that I have met musicians that do have that kind of training, and they have an appreciation for my timing and my understanding of the concept of playing on time. By placing the responsibility on yourself to learn this skill, I believe you can increase your personal musical experience and enhance your knowledge with other musicians who may be at a higher level of technical education than you.

It is one of the most basic forms of musical communication, and it can be easily overlooked. Talented musicians of all levels share this opinion, and they can quickly notice if someone is not knowledgeable about time.

ALTERNATE GUITAR TUNINGS

I would say that I have limited experience with alternative tunings because I don't use them all the time. That doesn't mean I have never used them or have zero experience with them, but I am not an expert. I am writing about them in this book because they can be an entertaining way to learn and express yourself. I can tell you that there are many ways to tune your guitar. The way that you will use on most gigs will be the standard tuning, and for me, it is the standard tuning a half step down.

Do you know what DADGAD means?
It means your guitar is tuned to those notes per string.

What about F5 tuning? FACFCF
I have learned one song to play in this tuning.

A more mainstream alternate tuning is the simplest one, in my opinion. Drop D. It's when you tune down the low E string a whole step, and that's it. You don't tune any other string differently. There are many songs for every alternate tuning, but this one is probably the most used and the most popular because it only requires adjusting the one string. If you want to add one song to your set, you can tune for it and tune back in between songs. If you're going to get into a more complex tuning and use it on a gig, it will make sense to do one of two things.

One is to learn to play more songs in the alternate tuning. This way, if you take the time it takes to tune five strings of your guitar to an alternate tuning, you can play and sing three or four songs in a row before you stop the show to tune all your strings back to standard tuning.

The second idea is to bring a second guitar already set up in the alternate tuning you want to use on one, two, or more songs. I wouldn't do this myself, but you will find what works for you.

Either way, if you do use alternate tunings and want to incorporate another guitar into your show to make it happen, make sure you are tuned up before you start and make sure that you plan your set so that doesn't interrupt your flow. You don't want beads of nervous sweat to trickle down your forchcad bccause of a mistake or something that you could have prevented with proper preparation.

PALM MUTING

Taking the palm of your pick hand and placing it lightly across the string or strings you want to pick is called palm muting. Once again, you can easily find a video online to show you what it looks like, but here is where I explain to you what the technique can do and what it means to me.

Like so many guitar techniques, this is made into reality by feel. If you overdo it, then it doesn't sound right. If you underdo it, then it doesn't sound right. The palm mute is another part of the fluid knowledge of the guitar, and it's another tool in the box that can help you express how you feel musically.

Any chord will do for this exercise. Hold your fret hand in position on the chord. Slightly press the side of your pick hand on the strings before you strike or pick the strings. This pressure from the side or palm of your hand will push the strings down. But how far down? That's part of the game here. My suggestion is to try a light to medium pressure, pushing down the side of your palm, and then picking or strumming over the chord. You will get it over time and with practice. It will become part of your natural way of playing guitar. One day you won't even consciously think about doing it unless you want to do it that way. It will start to interact with you when you change dynamics while you sing, and you will palm mute your strumming pick hand so that you can softly sing over your guitar. You will find yourself using multiple words at once and in the middle of a song to create a feel. A song will call for an open chord with a big voice, and then it will be followed by a palm-muted guitar chord with a softer voice. You will practice this idea repeatedly, and it will become a part of you.

A palm mute is a fundamental and commonly used part of guitar playing. It is probably overlooked and never talked about, but it makes such a dynamic difference that it can change a whole song for a Solo Acoustic Musician. It should be and will become part of your world of guitar playing. For those reading this book who have been playing guitar for a while, I think you should revisit your palm muting skills and find new songs or spots in old songs to use the palm mute for the desired effect that makes the song better.

 # SIDEBAR: LYRICS

As a Solo Acoustic Musician, I have spent time learning to play guitar, and spent time practicing my vocals. At a certain point in my career, I started to really think about what I was saying. What were the words I was singing? What were the messages that I was conveying? What did each song mean? And ultimately, was I okay with singing that song, or did I not want to say those words or create those feelings? The subject and content should matter to me. As a performer, I *should* care about what I am saying. It's not just a collection of random words (okay, maybe if it's a Red Hot Chili Peppers song, it is). It is a message and a specific set of subject matter, and it matters to me what I sing.

A lot can happen when we perform a song. We can create joy, or we can create sadness, and these are only two of the feelings that a song can try to impart to the listener. I believe the actual amount of energy that music can send out is infinite, because each person can and will react very differently to the same piece of music. Whether it's the rhythm, melody, or lyrics, a song can create a feeling in another person's soul. Memories are made, recalled, or forgotten after listening to music.

The beauty of lyrics is that you can often interpret songs any way you want, giving them a deeper meaning or a simple, literal one. It's all about what you need at the moment when you hear the song. For example, if you're going through heartache, you might feel the artist wrote the song for you, because it feels like it is speaking to your situation.

Songs are powerful things, and we should want to know what we are saying when we sing them. We must be responsible in some way for the message we send to other people when performing a song. Do you know the words to the songs that you sing? Do you know what they mean? Do they have more than one meaning? Do you understand the message of the lyrics that you are singing?

I will break down a few examples of lyrics and what they mean. These are songs that have been around a long time, and they may mean different things to other people. Many people may not care what the words are, or what they mean, because the lyrics aren't the only hook in the songs. People are just as stimulated by the beat, rhythm, and melody, regardless of the words or the meaning behind them.

As a Solo Acoustic Musician, do you want to know what you are singing and have a purpose? Let's explore this concept with a few songs and see what you think.

If you don't know what the lyrics to a song mean, then you can look them up. The first thing to do is google words you don't know and learn the definitions. You can dig deeper, if necessary, by using a site like urbandictionary.com for examples of current slang. Slang words are often used in lyrics of all genres or styles. Below are two examples of word definitions by using this website.

"The Joker" (Steve Miller Band, 1973)

Some people call me the space cowboy
Some call me the gangster of love
Some people call me Maurice
'Cause I speak of the pompatus of love
...

I'm a picker
I'm a grinner
I'm a lover
And I'm a sinner
I play my music in the sun
I'm a joker
I'm a smoker
I'm a midnight toker
I sure don't want to hurt no one
...
You're the cutest thing that I ever did see
I really love your peaches
Wanna shake your tree

Let's look at a few specific words in this song. You may already know what they mean, or you may not.

Space Cowboy (n.) Stoner, pothead, somebody who constantly smokes marijuana.
Example: "that guy is such a space cowboy."

Pompatus (n.) (multiple spellings) Splendor, magnificence, suave pageantry.
Pompatus is a nonsense word coined by Steve Miller in his hit single "The Joker" (1973). However, this was not the first time Miller used the word pompatus. He referenced an earlier song from 1972 called "Enter Maurice" from the album *Recall the Beginning: A Journey From Eden*.

Toker (n.) Someone who smokes marijuana. (See pothead.)

Let's also look at the phrase, "I really love your peaches/ Wanna shake your tree".

"Wanna shake your tree" means making those peaches (on the tree) move, which is a pretty straightforward analogy to sex. In this case, you can take peaches to mean breasts, and the tree is the rest of the body. Or you can take it to have a deeper meaning to the effect of, I like you, and I want to know all about you, till we are one. It was all about feeling good vibes, love, and peace in this era. The entire album gives off a happy vibe and this song is still played on the radio today.

The next song is full of words and phrases familiar to people from Australia. I am not from "down under," and I didn't know what some of the lyrics meant, so I looked them up, and this helped me understand more of the song's meaning.

"Down Under" (Men At Work, 1982)

Traveling in a fried-out Kombi
On a hippie trail, head full of zombie
I met a strange lady, she made me nervous
She took me in and gave me breakfast
And she said:
Do you come from a land down under?
Where women glow and men plunder
Can't you hear, can't you hear the thunder?
You better run, you better take cover
Buying bread from a man in Brussels
He was six foot four and full of muscle
I said, "Do you speak-a my language?"
He just smiled and gave me a Vegemite sandwich
And he said:
I come from a land down under
Where beer does flow and men chunder
Can't you hear, can't you hear the thunder?
You better run, you better take cover, ye-aah

Fried-out (adj.) Non-functioning or barely functioning.

Kombi (n.) A rear-engine, rear-wheel-drive van produced by Volkswagen from 1950-79, very popular in the '60s and early '70s, especially with surfers and hippies.

Zombie (n.) A potent batch of marijuana floating around Australia for a long time. People called it "Zombie Grass." The phrase "head full of Zombie" meant that you were very intoxicated from a substantial quantity of marijuana. I saw a SAM perform this song once, and he sang, "A head full of zombies." He must have read it from the lyric sheet wrong, or did not know what the words meant...

Down Under (n.) Australian slang for their home country. Example: "I'm going back down under, mate."

Chunder (n.) Aussie slang meaning to vomit. It originates from old seafaring days when sailors would get seasick and stick their heads out of the porthole in their cabin. They would shout "Watch under" as they did this, to warn people in lower cabins of the forthcoming vomit. Over the years, this evolved into "chunder."

Vegemite (n.) Vegemite is a fermented yeast spread that is pretty much a national institution in Australia. Some people love it and can't start the day without a piece of toast spread with Vegemite, and some go so far as to carry a small jar of it with them when they travel overseas. To make a Vegemite sandwich, you must toast two slices of bread and butter it. Then, you add just the right amount of spread, press the two slices together, and eat.

Here are a few other examples:

"Kokomo" (The Beach Boys, 1988)
Although the Beach Boys described Kokomo as a place "off the Florida Keys," there is no Kokomo in South Florida. There

is a Kokomo Charters in Sarasota, a Kokomo in Indiana, a Kokomo in the Fiji Islands, and a community named Kokomo in Hawaii. But the music video was filmed in Florida.

It's just another fun example of writing with imagination. Although Kokomo is a real word and a real place, it is not the place they sing about in their song.

"Sussudio" (Phil Collins, 1985)

According to Collins, this tune's lyrics tell the story of a boy who falls madly in love with a girl at his school but is unable to approach and talk to her. The song led to the birth of the slang term "sussudio," which refers to a girl whom a guy has a crush on but can't seem to talk to her. When asked what the meaning of the word was and if it meant anything to him, Collins said it was a meaningless word he just made up during the writing process. Who knows, maybe your next gibberish word could help you write a #1 song, too.

"Hotel California" (The Eagles, 1976)

This song has had more than one internet theory or urban legend about its meaning since it was written in 1976. I was stuck in traffic on the highway in Chicago in 1995 and listened for two hours as the radio DJs, and the people who called in, analyzed what they thought the song meant. It was very entertaining. They went through each line word by word and discussed the whole song in parts. There's a reason I haven't tried to explain "Hotel California." I want you to explore what you think it might mean. If you're going to read the lyrics and listen to the song, maybe you can figure out what the band is talking about and put the words into context.

I am sure that we could talk about these types of things all day, and I could probably write another book about this specifically. I can think of more songs with nonsense made-up words in them and more songs with slang words or adult content lyrics. I believe that you get my point. These are just a few examples to show how lyrics can influence what you think of a song. I know there are songs that I refuse to play because of what I think or what I have heard that the lyrics mean. It's my personal preference. I hope you find this helpful, and I hope you find songs with a message you want to share. When I believe in what I am singing, I think it's a more effective use of my energy as a performer. I think people react to my songs more honestly when I "feel" the message that I am sending out.

You should try it and see what happens. I believe you will see a difference once you take the time to analyze your song choices based on lyrical content. Don't just know the words to the songs you sing — know what they mean.

INTERVIEWS WITH SAMS

I. JIMMY SUVOY

Monday, June 21st, 2021, 2:30 PM
O'Keefe's Restaurant, Clearwater, FL

In the pages that follow, I will take you with me into a world full of Solo Acoustic Musicians and talk with them about their lives. My first stop along my journey is with Jimmy Suvoy.

I have known Jimmy for around ten years, and we even played a gig together long ago. He is an entertainer who likes to engage his audience when he plays songs and in between. Jimmy is a fun-loving guy who enjoys his life playing music and living in a Gulfside beach town. All he needs to do is walk down the street from his house to be on the beach at sunset. I know that he does this on his days off. I love the beach, too, and that's just one thing he and I have in common.

I consider Jimmy a friend and a colleague on my local music scene. There have been times when I needed someone to cover for me, or to play a gig that I wasn't available for, and he is on my short list of people to call. He has proven to be dependable and easy to work with when covering a gig. I get complimentary reviews from venues when I send him to play.

Once, when Jimmy arrived at a venue to cover a shift for me, the manager on duty turned out to be a guy that he had worked with many years before. So of course, they hit it off and reminisced about the beach bar Jimmy had played and Ralph managed, all those years ago. He covered my shift and helped me out, doing an excellent job, while also reuniting with a former connection. Jimmy was able to get gigs on his own calendar for future dates at that spot. It was a win for everyone involved.

When I reached out to him to be interviewed for this book, he was more than willing to meet up and talk. I was excited to get together with an old friend and talk about our lives as Solo Acoustic Musicians. We both arrived at a popular Irish restaurant in Clearwater, FL about ten minutes early and found our way to a back booth. Once we settled in, I turned on the recorder and we started talking...

Jimmy grew up around Pittsburgh, Pennsylvania, and started taking guitar lessons when he was ten years old, after his dad bought him an inexpensive guitar. About two years later, his dad bought him a nicer guitar after seeing how into it his son was. Jimmy was always into music, and it was also a big part of his family life, with musicians all over his family tree on both sides. Eventually, he joined an acoustic guitar band that played once a month in his Catholic church. They would perform for an acoustic mass instead of the organist. The group gained popularity and would play at different parishes in the area about once a month.

Jimmy recalls that he would stay in the background and strum along to the songs. He lacked confidence in his voice at that early age. He says that he can still remember playing those songs he learned at eleven and twelve years old.

Jimmy's family is also very much into athletics, and in junior high, he kind of put the guitar away and focused more on playing baseball, football, and volleyball. Basketball was his favorite. He would still play a little guitar here and there, though, and at family parties and get-togethers, there would always be a family band playing. He remembers sitting around the fire on camping trips and listening to people play music.

He learned from these family music experiences. He didn't play that much all through high school, but he did learn new songs and chord progressions when he could.

After high school, he received a scholarship to play basketball in college, and although he brought his guitar with him and it was in his bedroom, he didn't have much time to dedicate to music. He discovered that a few of the guys on the basketball team liked to sing together, and they joined a talent show at the college, singing an Earth, Wind, and Fire song. They won.

Life after college didn't allow for much more focus on music, as Jimmy got married and started having kids. He got a regular job to support his family, though he still had a guitar and would even play songs for his kids from time to time. He remembers camping trips where he would bring his guitar and play around the fire. When his kids were in high school, Jimmy started going to open mics around Pittsburgh. He says that he didn't like it at first, but that one of the hosts at an event near his house was very encouraging towards him. The guy kept telling Jimmy to keep coming back and that he would get better. "We all like you here." By this time, Jimmy was already in his mid- to late thirties. He had never really taken music seriously up to this point.

Eventually, he played his first paying gig — when he was forty-five years old. He was still in Pittsburgh, but was about to make a life change and move to Florida. Jimmy is now sixty-one and has been living in Florida for the last fifteen years.

When he arrived, he started a bartending job at one of the beach hotels. Within a month of his arrival, a Solo Acoustic Musician was playing at the bar where Jimmy was working, and they started talking. Jimmy told the guy he played, and the other musician said he was always on the lookout for new people to cover a gig if he needed to play with his band. This musician, who was on a break, invited Jimmy to go up on stage and play a few songs. So, Jimmy got up on stage in his bartender uniform and played some songs.

A few hotel managers gathered to watch him. When he was done and back behind the bar, the other musician told him that he was good and could give him some bookings right away. Jimmy had been in Florida less than a month.

The managers who were watching were also impressed. The one in charge of booking the music at the hotel tiki bar was present and approached Jimmy about playing there. The hotel had an active gig calendar, and the guy started getting Jimmy into the rotation right away. This led to him playing all the time at the beach hotel, where he was also a bartender. Things were going well for Jimmy until the GM of the hotel called him into the office one day. He explained that he didn't want Jimmy to bartend *and* play music at the hotel. He would have to choose between the two. Jimmy decided to turn in his apron and continue playing music at the tiki beach bar. I can't blame him; I would have made the same choice.

He played there a couple of times a week, but needed to find some more income. Right across the street from the hotel, a bar that was going to have live music was under construction. Jimmy met the owner, who hired him as a daytime bartender. He created a title for himself as the "Guitartender." He would sit behind the bar with his acoustic guitar and play two or three songs, and then he would announce to the patrons that he was coming around to replenish their drinks. After refilling everyone's drinks, he would sit back down, play more songs, and repeat the process. He told me he was "crushing it" on tips by working like this, taking requests and playing songs for people.

He was also playing gigs in the bar at night and started hosting an open mic night there' which lasted for just over eight years. That is a good run and a successful open mic. He was still very new to the area, and this was where he met local musicians that he still knows today. Going to and performing at the open mic was a path to getting a gig at the bar, so many local musicians would come down and play songs to "audition."

These two gigs were life-changing situations for Jimmy, and they both happened at practically the same time, right when he moved to the Clearwater area. Before long, Jimmy was making a solid living and playing consistently at bars along the beach. By the end of 2006, he had given up bartending entirely and was playing music full time as a Solo Acoustic Musician. He worked gigs five or six nights a week, with one or two afternoon slots on his calendar. He became well known on Clearwater beach. This resort town with tourists gave him a lot of new people to perform in front of every week.

I asked Jimmy about a specific piece of gear he uses right now. He has a battery-powered speaker that I had seen him using in some Facebook posts, and I was curious about it. He told me it's a Bose S1 speaker/amp combo with two jacks, one for his guitar and the other for his microphone. It has Bluetooth, so he can use his phone to play music when he goes on breaks. He says it's useful for beach and boat gigs.

I gave him a tip about a catamaran boat that hires SAMs for sunset cruises. His battery-powered Bose S1 combo would be a perfect P.A. in that situation. When he bought the S1, he looked for something compact to use at home for practice and playing gigs. He says that it does a wonderful job for most of his restaurant and bar gigs. He also has a couple of larger speakers that he can add, though, when he is playing somewhere that might require more sound coverage. This extra equipment would most likely be an outside gig where he must point speakers in more than one direction.

He lives in Indian Rocks Beach, south of Clearwater, and his battery-powered speaker came in handy during the shutdowns. A mutual friend called Jimmy and talked about how everyone would be doing a drive-by birthday celebration for another friend. They were going to honk their horns, and people were even going to bring lawn chairs to celebrate together by placing their chairs a certain distance apart. Jimmy drives a Mustang convertible, and he thought to himself that he could sit on the top of the backseat and use his S1 to play music remotely from his car for this birthday celebration. The S1's battery pack could last for hours. He was turning his car into a movable stage.

When he arrived, the birthday girl started crying and was overwhelmed by the gesture that he was going to sing for her birthday. She has been a long-time friend and fan of Jimmy's music. He was only going to play two songs and then go back home, but people responded in such a way that he stayed and played longer. People were walking by and throwing money in the backseat of his car. People were going to the balconies of their condominiums to watch and listen to him perform. He ended up playing for two hours from the back of his car.

Other people heard about what he was doing and reached out to him to play in their neighborhoods. This type of show became a popular thing, and he was doing shows five days a week from his car all up and down the nearby beach towns. He would park in the host's driveway, and all the neighbors would sit in their yards. He described the convertible top going back as being like a curtain going up for the start of a traditional show. We joked that he needed a fog machine and some more lights other than just the headlights. People were generous, and he was making good money playing these pop-up events for tip money. He even got creative with his tip can. He used a mop handle inside a pool noodle to extend it away from the car by four feet. At the end was a rope with a Kool-Aid pitcher tied to it. Word of mouth spread, and he was staying busy.

During this time, his regular gig venues were closed down. As businesses adapted to delivery or carryout only, Jimmy adapted, too. He reached out to a person he knew who owned a pizza shop and pitched the idea of playing music from his car in the parking lot. So now he is doing his driveway concerts in a pizza shop parking lot. In my opinion, this is a very creative way to adapt to a stressful time. People were coming and going from picking up their food, and some of them tailgated at their vehicles in the parking lot. The owner even offered prizes as incentives for people to tip Jimmy.

The guitar he is playing right now is a Martin 00CXAE. It's a thin composite body with black matte color, and it's very lightweight and has Fishman electronics installed. He says he loves the way it plays and sounds. He went further to say that he always uses the Nanoweb Phosphor Bronze eleven-gauge Elixir brand guitar strings.

Jimmy likes to keep a tambourine handy on stage. He will offer it to people in the audience for them to play along with the music. He likes to include children when he does this, and says it gets him extra dollars in his tip can. Everyone has fun watching the kids dance and play the tambourine.

He told me a story about a recent gig where a group of girls from Iowa were in town on vacation to celebrate one of their birthdays. He engaged the audience by leading them in singing the birthday song, followed by getting the birthday girl on stage with him to play the tambourine. The crowd ate it up and cheered her on, creating a lot of energy. I told him that I thought this was a creative way of working the crowd and engaging the audience. It adds a certain amount of entertainment value beyond just standing there and playing songs.

I asked Jimmy to tell me about a gig where something went wrong and what happened. He proceeded to tell me about a time when he arrived at a venue and realized he didn't have a mic stand with him. He had left the house in a hurry and somehow forgot to grab it. With no time to go home and get one, he had to improvise. After asking the staff for help, he ended up with a mop handle, a table umbrella base, and some duct tape. He stuck the mop handle down into the base and duct-taped it. He also duct-taped his microphone to the top of the handle. Jimmy is six foot four, and I was laughing as I pictured this tall guy leaning over this short mop handle in my mind. He told me he lifted it onto some bricks or something so that it wasn't as bad as it could have been. Another SAM, a local friend, brought Jimmy an actual microphone stand right around the end of his second set. This replacement stand helped make the rest of his gig better, and he said he still has pictures of himself singing on the mop stick mic stand. He also had another experience where his guitar input jack malfunctioned and reached out to someone who could bring him a guitar to use for the gig. He later replaced the jack at the guitar shop. As a Solo Acoustic Musician, sometimes we must adjust on the fly when things go wrong.

We talked about showing up and finding out the venue is double-booked. It can be awkward when you get to a gig, and another musician is setting up, or vice versa. Do you play? Do they play? Do you figure it out yourself between the two of you, or do you talk with and involve the manager on duty? He explained that the coolest solution to this problem that he has seen so far is to have the two musicians play together or split the gig. This scenario could mean that they team up like a duo or take turns playing sets.

He talked about a time that this happened to him, and the owner suggested that they play together and that he would pay them both for the gig. Because of a severe difference in style and the fact that the other musician played along with backing tracks, Jimmy decided that they should take turns, playing sets one after the other. He said it worked out well and that the owner was happy, the other musician was happy, and of course, he was pleased with the end of the gig. I know from personal experience that it can be a total bummer to show up and not get paid because of a double booking. This sounded like it worked out for everyone involved, and I would even encourage you to try to remember to use this tactic in the future if you find yourself in this situation. We both agreed that it was rare for an owner to step up and offer a solution that involved paying both musicians. But it does happen.

Pro Tip: *Follow up your booking conversations by backing up your detailed confirmations in emails or texts. That way, you can always access the information on your phone if there is a discrepancy when you get to the gig.*

Jimmy has written several cool songs over the years and has one original that people request often. It's a well-crafted and intelligent song that is funny as well. It has a controversial part, so I am not sharing its name here. I am sure you can find it if you look. He told me that his writing happens in spurts. He described moments of inspiration where he would write a batch of songs all at once. They just seemed to come to him. He said that he had never really had to work hard at writing a song. It just happens.

Currently, he has a batch of songs written and will write one more, when it happens, for a new album that he is calling *What Could Go Wrong?* The last song will be the title track.

He explained his personal philosophy about life to me. He looks at the worst-case scenario and the best-case scenario, believing reality will be somewhere in the middle, but if he can manage the worst-case scenario, he perseveres. This belief is the concept behind his new song idea. If he can handle the worst-case scenario if it happens, he can eliminate the fear of taking the chance and moving forward in life, even if there is a risk of failure. Any apprehension is gone. If it goes wrong, he is okay. He is already prepared for that to happen. Then at the same time, he thinks about what can go right. Can he manage the success? He has applied this tactic to many decisions in his life.

We moved on, and I asked him for a personal perspective on performing. He responded that he draws a line or creates a fence, and he can quickly put other musicians on one side or the other. The dividing line is this: Are you there for the people, or are you there for yourself? He knows a musician who will flip the crowd the middle finger if he doesn't get applause after a particular song. I was shocked when he told me this, and I had to stop the interview for a second to make sure that he wasn't joking. If you play forty songs a day, after how many songs do you not receive applause because people are talking or eating? So, was this musician playing his gig for the people or himself?

Jimmy talked about another musician who gets upset if people talk during his show. Jimmy believes that you are there for the audience. They are not there for you. The audience did not pay fifty dollars for a ticket to see you play. The gigs he was referencing are bar and restaurant shows.

Still, Jimmy considers himself an entertainer when he is on stage. As I think I know what he means, I will say that we are musicians and play an instrument, but when we get onto the stage, we can become something completely different. As an entertainer, you will find ways to engage the crowd and make something happen beyond just standing there playing songs. He reminds me of the tambourine he uses as an icebreaker and then tells me how the Pittsburgh Steelers "terrible towel" hanging on his mic stand gets attention. People from the home cities of rival football teams will interact with him, and it helps open dialogue.

He has a black and yellow floor fan that he uses on gigs, and he put a Steelers sticker on it. People will see it and say, "Look, it's a Steeler fan. Get it?" If someone walks by in a Cleveland Browns football team shirt, Jimmy will say something like, "Oh, you're from Cleveland, that's too bad." It's a good way to break the ice, as long as it's done as a fun, teasing type of interaction. You have to walk that fine line, though. You don't want to insult people.

This kind of banter can open communication with a stranger in the audience, which can lead to more banter and song requests, leading to more tips and fun throughout the gig. He has added little battery-operated candles that change colors to catch people's eye, which he puts around his tip can. You can get them at a dollar store for cheap. His tip can is made of transparent plastic, so the lights attract people's attention. He told me that the little things sometimes will draw attention and connect you with someone in the audience.

Jimmy also enjoys telling stories about the songs, whether he wrote them or not. Father's Day was the day before our interview. He had announced to the crowd that night that he thought the Harry Chapin song "Cat's in the Cradle" was the best Father's Day song ever, and that he would probably be playing it a few times. We agreed that we would usually never repeat a song at a gig unless someone made a special request. This example of a holiday was a good reason to play a song more than once. He added that you can repeat it later when you are playing a gig from six to ten in the evening, and you have already played a song in the first set. If someone came up to you at nine-thirty and asked for a song you already played at six-thirty, you wouldn't say, "Sorry, I can't. I already played it earlier." That makes sense to me. Especially since most, if not all, of the audience is probably different people, not the ones you played the song for three hours ago.

Jimmy will book gigs in Pittsburgh when he goes back to visit family and friends. It's fun for his fans there to hang out with him while he is in town. Sometimes he "tours," working his way through different cities to and from Pittsburgh. He will pick towns where he has friends or places he wants to visit, and sometimes he will book a gig along the way.

One time he was going through Savannah, GA, and stopped at a bar for food. He intended to give the owner his card for future reference and to try to book a gig on his next trip through town. The guy says, "Can you play tonight? I need someone for tonight." Jimmy agreed and played a gig that night.

On another trip north, he stopped in a small town outside Charlotte, NC, and found his way to an open mic less than ten minutes from his hotel room. Jimmy met other musicians there and went to hang out with people afterward. He had a fun night of jamming with them and making new friends. I have experienced nights like these, and it was fun to hear him talk about being adventurous on his road trip. Leaving his hotel room and going to an open mic ended up being a great night.

Picking out songs for gigs is a process — Jimmy likes to stick to songs he likes, but he takes requests and tries to learn songs that people also want to hear. He also tries to pick out songs that other people don't play. I try to do this myself, but overlaps happen. I make it a point not to deliberately choose the same cover songs as other people I see playing out.

Jimmy enjoys it when someone from the audience comes up to him and says that they like a song he just played and that nobody does that song. I agree that it adds something unique to your show as a SAM if you are playing songs that all the other musicians on your scene aren't playing. There are a lot of "standard" songs that people request from SAMs all the time, and it's fun to play some that aren't the typical choices. When people ask him what kind of music he plays, he will tell them he plays an eclectic mix. It even says that on his business card.

Sitting down with an old friend in an old familiar place was a terrific way to start this series of interviews. Jimmy is honest, genuine, and a fun person to talk to about being a Solo

Acoustic Musician. His stories about his life were fun to listen to, and his abilities as a SAM are a blessing for anyone in the audience when he performs. He has an energy and a positivity about him that is contagious. I can't wait to hear more of his stories down the road; I know that we will stay in touch. I am sure that sometime soon, when I have a night off, I will find Jimmy playing down at the beach. I just hope he doesn't try to get me to play the tambourine or dance.

You can find Jimmy online at jimmysuvoy.com; check him out and listen to some songs.

II. BRIAN LENESCHMIDT

Tuesday, June 22nd, 2021, 2 PM
Ferg's Sports Bar & Grill, St. Petersburg, FL

At the end of this conversation, Brian Leneschmidt and I noticed that the place had filled up all around us. We were in our own little world during the second of my SAM interviews, talking about a topic that we both were incredibly enthusiastic about, and time passed around us. But now we were noticing a lot of Tampa Bay Rays shirts.

As we headed out to the parking lot, we realized the team had an evening game, and people had arrived downtown. Founded in 1992, Ferg's is right across the street from the Tropicana stadium where the Rays play baseball and is the official gathering spot for fans. We chose to meet there at 2 PM on a Tuesday because it would probably be slower between lunch and dinner service. And indeed, it was quiet until about 4 o'clock, when it started packing up in anticipation of a busy game night at the bar. When we arrived, we had a side room all to ourselves. So, we ordered drinks and snacks and started talking about life as a Solo Acoustic Musician.

I jumped right in by asking Brian when he started playing guitar, and about his beginnings. He was fourteen years old and living in Cheyenne, WY, when he began to play. His dad played a little bit of guitar and encouraged Brian. He recalls that he wished he would have started even earlier. When Brian was fourteen and MTV came out, he loved all the rock 'n' roll videos and wanted to play guitar. Of course, his dad taught him the basic chords and helped him get started.

It just so happened that Brian's neighbor was a guitar teacher, so he started taking lessons from him. That teacher became somewhat of a mentor to Brian; the lessons lasted for a little more than a year. Brian wanted to learn AC/DC and blues-based rock 'n' roll, and this teacher could show him all the things he wanted to know. He taught him how to play pentatonic scales and build solos. Brian says that it was great that his teacher was right next door, so he could teach him all the stuff he wanted to know back then. He was learning rock 'n' roll licks from famous songs.

As Brian developed his guitar abilities and started high school, he began to play with a band. He also had a job working for the city as a gravedigger throughout his twenties. He worked for a cemetery for almost a decade and played gigs on the weekends with his blues band. He quit the city job to play music full-time when he was about twenty-seven years old.

His band at the time had signed with a manager that ended up being a joke, meaning the person was not a professional or proper manager. There was nothing funny about it. I have heard similar stories from other musicians about failed management relationships. Brian didn't let that discourage him, though. He had already decided that he wanted to play music for a living. But the group started changing, and eventually disbanded altogether. At that point, he even considered hanging it up as a profession, but to his surprise, someone asked him if he would play acoustic at a bar. He had never played a solo gig. I asked him what it was like the first time. He said, "I got through it somehow." I know it must have been weird to go from having your friends on stage with you to being completely alone in front of a crowd of people.

He remembered that he barely had enough material. He was used to playing guitar solos with the band, and at his solo acoustic show, he had to play and sing songs straight up with no other instrumentation. He called it a "plug in and play" situation. Then one of his friends bought a looper pedal, and Brian thought it was cool, so he got one, too, and started doing more acoustic gigs. Brian has always done both band and the solo gigs ever since. He keeps a full calendar balanced between the two. Usually, he likes to have one band gig a week, on a Saturday night. Our focus though, was talking about his solo gigs and what his experiences are from that perspective.

Brian said he only ever uses the looper pedal to create a rhythm guitar part he can play lead guitar over. This is the purest and most basic use of the looper. He also uses this technique for an intro sometimes. I like that he keeps it simple, and we talked about the last time I saw him play. He was playing and singing a song, and then he went into a guitar solo over the verse chords. It was simple, tasteful, and an excellent guitar solo. He added that he doesn't save any loops, which means if he needs one for a song, he builds it from scratch every time.

We both had the same thought about how sometimes people in the audience think we are playing over pre-recorded tracks. It's something that we pick up on, and can even be asked about by an audience member. Brian will take a minute to explain what he is doing and make a loop for the person right there on the spot. I think this is an excellent way to show the audience what we are doing on stage. He said he has demonstrated building loops between songs to show someone what he is doing with the pedal.

"This is how this works. It's all live music. There's nothing pre-recorded." Brian has had to say this to people in the past when they don't seem to understand what he is doing. He says he's good at setting up his loops, but can mess it up sometimes. It's live music, and mistakes can happen. He says, "Just wait for me to screw it up, and then you'll know it's not a track." He also tells his crowds, "If you pay enough attention to me, you're going to hear a song sometime in the next half hour or so, and there will be something that isn't going to be just perfectly synced." Most people probably wouldn't catch it unless they were listening for it.

Pro Tip: *Stoke the fire! Learn something new on the guitar and find a way to work it into a song, not just your practice routine.*

Since we had been talking about an effects pedal, I asked Brian to tell me about the other gear he is currently using. He said that he is old-fashioned and uses EV fifteens for his solo gigs. The reference to "fifteens" means that he uses speakers with fifteen-inch speakers in them. He is not using powered speakers, and has a powered mixer. He explains that he can also use the EV brand fifteens for a band gig. His pedalboard is nothing more than his looper, a chorus pedal (which he uses a few times per gig), and an EQ pedal in case he has to deal with any particularly awful feedback issues. He mostly keeps this pedal flat. He plays Taylor guitars, and he has older models. Currently, he uses nanoweb Elixir twelve-gauge guitar strings. Brain says to check out juststrings.com for deals on strings and for single strings, which he keeps on hand in case he breaks one on a gig.

Brian is forty-nine years old, which means he has played guitar for thirty-five years. As he became a better guitarist himself, he began teaching lessons. Although he has done some teaching in the Tampa Bay area, he taught more when he lived in Cheyenne. He didn't have as many gig opportunities in Wyoming as in Florida, so he supplemented his income with lessons. He would gig a few nights a week when he lived there and give eight or ten students lessons every week. These students would fill his Mondays and Tuesdays.

He said he never wanted to teach guitar, and I saw the wheels turning as this somehow transported us back to high school. He played the horn, but quit because he wanted to play guitar. He regrets that, and said that he should have continued because he would probably still be able to read music proficiently. In his senior year of high school, he took a music theory class, and about two weeks into it, he realized that he didn't need it to graduate.

He said he didn't like school and would watch the clock all day because he couldn't wait to get out. He admitted he was not motivated and was a terrible student. He never flunked any classes, but he didn't apply himself. All he wanted to do was play guitar.

Brian said that he never learned modes and things like that correctly because he quit the music theory course. Admittedly he was probably playing some of that stuff, but he didn't know the how and why, and wouldn't be able to explain it to someone else because he didn't understand it all. He also referenced building chords beyond the basic stuff that we first learned. He jokingly says that he knew some of the "expensive" (meaning advanced, jazzy/beyond beginner level) chords, but he didn't know the how and why.

Fast forward some years later and Brian was having a conversation with a drummer friend, and worried that he didn't have enough gigs on the calendar. To which his friend replied, "You need to teach." Although Brian confessed to his friend that he couldn't teach, that he wouldn't know what he was doing, the friend somehow convinced him to try, and he relented.

His strategy to start with was to find beginners for students. As he began teaching, he realized that it was the best thing he had ever done. It helped him out, and he became a better musician. Some of his students would have questions for him that maybe he didn't have good answers for at the time. So Brian told himself that if he was going to teach guitar, he would have to make up for decisions he had previously made. He gave himself a crash course in more advanced music theory. Because of this, Brian said that he learned more by teaching than he probably taught. It helped his playing and how he thinks about playing the guitar.

He doesn't consider himself a great teacher, but he loves to do it. He doesn't teach music the way it is supposed to be taught. He has ways to cheat and knows when to play a specific scale or mode. He can teach someone to use a Mixolydian mode at a jam session even if they don't know what key it's supposed to be. He says that there are all kinds of ways to look at music and that you don't have to think like a mathematician to understand. He's never going to teach music in school, but what he teaches is practical, and it works.

Brian moved to St. Petersburg, Florida, in the Tampa Bay area, in 2011. It was a significant culture shift from Cheyenne, Wyoming. I remember when I started to see a new name popping up on calendars around town and on social media posts from venues that promote their musicians. The new guy in town was developing a buzz, and the word was quickly traveling the peninsula about his guitar playing.

When he was a new arrival and just settling in, he met people who took him out to all the open jams. He says he did two years of networking in two months, and met all kinds of musicians. He went out to jams every night and was introduced to all the local players. He commented that he felt like he was about to jump into a shark tank because of the outstanding players who were there. It would be a different scene from where he grew up in Wyoming, based on the population and tourism.

It seems like there is always a new musician in our town. Brian said that you don't have to be the best player that's ever walked the planet. But if you can be dependable, do a good job, not get drunk, and not be a jerk, you can stay busy. I must add that I think those rules to live by apply everywhere. He admits that it's not always easy, and we all have ups and downs. This lifestyle can be frustrating sometimes, but it's possible to make a living being a Solo Acoustic Musician.

I changed the subject and asked Brian how he picks out songs to add to his repertoire. He explained that he doesn't want to learn songs unless he likes them, and he doesn't pick songs for the crowd. I thought it was great to hear him be so honest. Brian says that what he does musically when in SAM mode is quite different from playing his electric guitar with his band. He wants to be mellow and relaxed. He says that he is not a party MC when he is solo. He has found places to do his SAM act that appreciate his talent and approach to the music. He is much more aggressive and in-your-face with his musical choices and styles when he is with his band.

He added that it is essential to find out if he can sing the song. So one of the first things he does after he decides that he likes a song and wants to learn it is to try to sing it. He talked about changing the key or changing the song to fit the way he can sing it. He may wind up creating a unique version. What's interesting about this part of the process is that he won't listen to the original artist's version of the song for two or three years. Then when he hears it again, he often realizes that he is doing the music nothing like the original version.

Brian's mode of transportation is a Dodge minivan, and he loves its versatility. He said that he can comfortably carry all his gear. He primarily performs in places close to home but does occasionally have road trips here in Florida that will take him more than an hour from home, and the van is a comfortable way to travel.

Pro Tip: *For your singing voice: Hydration. Hydration. Hydration. — Brian Leneschmidt*

Brian said he could probably write a chapter on throat trouble.

He said that he has had a terrible time with his voice since moving to Florida, that he is allergic to everything that grows here and has reflux issues that he didn't know he had. He told me it's called silent reflux and that many singers get it. After visiting an ENT doctor and getting a scope procedure done, he learned all about what was going on between the reflux and the postnasal drip due to allergies. He said that he ended up with nodules off and on. Then he finally hemorrhaged a vocal cord and ended up having surgery. The doctor also worked on his sinuses at the same time. I interjected that this sounded like a nightmare! He agreed and told me that he considered quitting and never singing again.

As working SAMs, we must go to work on gigs to pay the bills. Brian said it's easy to be macho and tough it out and push through, singing sixty gigs a month because we have to do it. We're just going to kill ourselves on the gig and get up in the morning and not be able to talk. Throw a cup of coffee down and grind through it again because we're tough pros, but that's the absolute worst thing to do. When your voice isn't good, it's telling you something. Because if you keep forcing those vocal cords to vibrate together when they're not in good shape, day after day, and you're only taking one or two days off at a time, it's not enough time to heal. Your voice might come back, but you are not healed properly. You will have problems like vocal nodules or polyps. It's a common thing, and when he became that person, he did a lot of research. It's incredible how many people go through this. It was almost harder to find examples of singers who hadn't had these problems. He read their stories and related to them and what they went through.

Brian thinks singers have to watch their dairy intake. For example, don't eat a bunch of pizza if you have to sing that day. He said that everybody is different, and he has learned what works for him. If you are going to be a full-time singer, your voice has to be your top priority. Even if you have a week off from gigs, your voice has still got to be your number one priority. Proper sleep, proper diet, rest, and hydration!

I compared what he said to being an athlete who has injured their knee and taken time to rest and heal, only to be brought back too soon and re-aggravate the same injury, only now it's worse, and they will be out of commission even longer. The amount of time and effort to heal and return will be magnified. As a singer, I would not want that to happen to me. He told me that he went through that scenario every week for five or six years. He was still playing two hundred and forty gigs a year. He didn't stop. He even said that his wife told him that he needed to slow down. I understood this drive. He had to play his guitar and sing, even when he was not healthy and could have used a break. I have pushed myself many times in the past, and I think I have found more balance in this area at this point in my life. I guess Brian learned and understands his body's need for rest and healing.

Brian told me that he goes through periods where he doesn't write, and then something will click. He also has a friend who he bounces lyrics off, and they help each other write songs. Brian said that writing is fun for him. He talked about the fact that he listens to everything. He likes metal, opera, blues, jazz, heavy stuff, and mellow stuff. Depending on where his head is, he may have ideas for songs that may not be anything that he would ever use or play because they wouldn't fit into his repertoire. Writing is tricky for him; he can't just "turn it on," as some people can.

Brian said he doesn't do anything special for his tip and merchandise setup. He has a box from the hardware store that holds CDs, and he has a sign that advertises them. The little box was a twenty-dollar purchase, and he had the sign professionally printed. He even says that CDs will sell at gigs, and don't let anybody tell you that people don't buy CDs anymore, because they do.

When I brought up promotion, he said that whether you like social media or not, you have to use it for gigs. He says that he has a great website that nobody probably sees because they won't go to musicians' or bands' websites. People will go on social media and other boards that promote local events and happenings. He confided in me that he doesn't like having to maintain multiple social media presences, but knows we need them for our jobs as SAMs. He finally decided to create a social media presence separate from his musical life. Now he has more fun and feels that he gets way more traction from his gig flyers and postings than before. He spends less time on all the sites, too, which works better for him.

He said that booking gigs is the hardest part of being a SAM. Everybody has a unique way of doing it. He claimed that he doesn't have a good demo or video reel, and that most of his new clients come from references and word of mouth. He mentioned a venue that he has been playing for years now and thanked me for helping him get in. He has done an excellent job and is still working with that venue. Brian said that many of his gigs have come from similar situations, and through networking with other musicians in the area.

He described the music scene in our county as an awesome group of people (and I agree). It has been fantastic for him. There is not a lot of dirty competition; people are cool with each other, and supportive. For example, if there is a crappy venue owner who is bouncing checks to musicians, they will all use social media to warn each other to watch out for that person. We help each other get gigs. He added that his experience here may not be typical, because he felt that he has been cared for very well here. We all go through difficulties with our schedules because venues close, and other variables can cause us to lose gigs.

Brian's advice on getting gigs: Once you get a little bit established in your area and can make a good video, do it. Don't make a demo CD to drop off at bars. Those days are long gone. Use your social media platforms or a direct email to send your video around. Also, don't take gigs for cheap. Don't drag the collective pay rate for your area down even if you're new. We all know you want to get your foot in the door, but you shouldn't play a gig for a low rate or for free.

He also said not to go in acting like you are the best thing ever and asking for ridiculous money, but neither should you go in acting meek and looking desperate. We both agreed that texts or emails are pretty much a necessity these days, to be used in confirming all the details about a gig: the date, the time, the pay, etc.

Brian told me that he doesn't like a lot of dead air between songs, and he doesn't want to talk a lot or be chatty on the mic either. He will move on to play the next song reasonably quickly. He said that he enjoys playing at a local wine bar because it's like a listening room. The customers there are usually quiet and paying attention to the music. There are no TVs, and the musician is a focal point for the evening's entertainment. People come there to hear good music and to drink good wine. Of course, he admitted that every room is different, and he tries to read a room as best he can. That is an art form all its own.

Brian tends to guide the room through the show with his song selections more than the words he has to say. So, if he feels it's getting too sleepy, he will play a peppy, up-tempo song. On the other hand, if people are getting too rowdy, he will try to calm them down with his next song choice.

I brought up the weather, and we discussed the difference between Cheyenne, Wyoming, and where he lives now in Florida. He said that you don't play outside in Cheyenne very often. Maybe a special event or outdoor festival in the summer or something like that. But pretty much every other gig is indoors. In Cheyenne, they have snow and freezing weather. Here in Florida, we have rain, especially in the summer rainy season. I asked Brian if he had any secret things he does to deal with the weather situations we encounter here, and he said, "Carry tarps!" and laughed.

He said that the one thing that blows his mind about venues, especially venues that have live music every day of the week, is that they will spend upwards of eighty thousand dollars or more on their music budget, but not build anything to put the musicians in, like a stage with a roof, walls, or flaps. He said that sometimes they'll put you in the worst possible position, where you are not even doing any good for them. I immediately thought of places that I play where I am not set up in what I would think would be the best position to be seen and heard. He told me that sometimes he wants to speak to the manager or venue owner and tell them that they don't know their job. "Please, let me help you with this — let me tell you where I should be setting up and playing so that you can get the most bang for your buck after hiring me to entertain your patrons. You are buying my time, and I want to provide you with a quality product." While he was describing this fictional conversation, I was laughing and nodding in agreement, because I feel the same way and would love to say things like this to some venue owners I know.

Even if the venue setup is right, sometimes the gig isn't. Recently an agent was trying to book him for a Fourth of July party at a biker bar, and quoting Brian, he said, "I'll do it, but they aren't going to be happy. I'm not a classic rock band." He didn't think they would know any of the songs he would play, or that it would be a good fit musically.

I asked him if he remembered when a specific venue we knew first opened, and how they would have the musician set up at the far end of the pool, away from the bar. That was a logistical nightmare, and I wouldn't play there unless they let me set up my gear under or by the roof and closer to the bar crowd. Being on the water and that far from safety with a pool between me and a dry place was a horrible idea. He agreed, and we both played there — once management changed where we could set up. I told him that I didn't think I had ever had a conversation with another musician who was as passionate as me about this issue. I mentioned another venue where they spent money to tear down the old building and build a completely brand-new spot, from the first floor up to the third floor. Then they put the musician as far away from the building as possible, with no cover or anything. We both were in shock at the lack of forethought, considering they had had live music performers for years previously. Spending all that money on a new building and then not even addressing the position or including the musicians' staging area in the plan was ridiculous.

Another example of lousy placement Brian brought up is when a venue puts you on the other side of the building from the bar patrons who want to hear the loud music. They tell you to turn it up so everyone can listen to you, and then you end up angering and alienating all the tables in front of you who are trying to have a quiet dinner. I have been in this situation, too, and it is no fun. He said, "Nobody wants to sit there and be blasted by the music while trying to eat their food."

I asked Brian to share a story of when something went wrong at a gig, he told me about a drunk lady who approached him and asked him if she could sing a song. Of course, he was polite to her, but also told her no. She continued saying that she knew the words. "But I know the words. I know the words." Then he told me that after she repeated herself a few more times, she just fell out, right on the deck of the tiki bar. So now it's an inside joke with him and some of his musician buddies. They will be hanging out, and one of them will say, "I know the words." He admitted that he sees that kind of thing all the time.

Brian talked to me about the balance of dealing with venue owners or managers and how he has tried not to become cynical after years of drunken bar business. Between drunk customers and the power struggles for control with management, it can be a frustrating existence that can wear someone down over time. He tried not to sound negative when he said that we, as musicians, are looked down on sometimes, even perceived as a problem for some managers. Some of them don't want to deal with us, let alone be nice to us. Finding that middle ground where you don't get jaded is vital for longevity in this lifestyle. It's essential to be able to put up with some things while at the same time being able to stick up for yourself.

He said that he tries to fly under the radar, meaning that he swoops in, plays the gig, and swoops out. He doesn't like to be right in the management's face. He even went as far as to say that "the less you know about me being there, then the better it's probably going to go." They don't have to worry about him or focus on him, and they know he will be there and is reliable.

A big part of Brian's success as a Solo Acoustic Musician is that he is a super nice guy. We discussed being double-booked, and he confessed that it seems like he always gets the short end of the stick in those situations. When a manager has made the mistake of booking two musicians for the same shift, they almost always ask Brian to concede the gig. We agreed that it's probably because they know he will accept it and deal with the situation nicely. On the other hand, the other musician might get mad and initiate a confrontation.

Brian understands the balance between confidence and arrogance, and chooses to navigate situations like this maturely. I believe that it's an integral part of developing long-lasting relationships with venues or clients. Double bookings don't happen often, and how a SAM deals with them is vital to their future relationship with that client. I can appreciate that Brian doesn't get upset about or take it personally, that he acts like a professional when dealing with a crappy situation.

Brian is a very humble person and it blows his mind that he gets to make a living by playing his guitar and singing. It blows *my* mind how humble he is, because he is an amazingly talented performer. He told me that his advice for someone starting and trying to be a full-time musician for a living is that it is a genuine business. If you can do it, you are just as legitimate a businessperson as anyone else. This gig is your job. You are a professional now. Act like it. You worked extremely hard to get to do this for a living. It's a risk to leave the "normal" or "typical" job market and start your own business. You must invest your time improving your skills and invest some money into your business. You need to buy business cards, build a website, get gear and sell yourself to get gigs. He talked about supplying a service for the venue or client just like any other business. Thinking like this is an excellent perspective to develop, because some people don't see being a musician as an "actual" job.

I have known Brian for quite a few years now, but we don't get to hang out much because we are both playing gigs simultaneously. I believe the last time I saw him was in Safety Harbor, FL. It was a two-gig day for me, and I was in between gigs when I popped into a local restaurant for a salad and just happened to catch part of his set. It was nice to see him, hear him play a few songs, and we were even able to talk a little bit when he went on a break. When I decided to do this second book, I immediately thought to call Brian and ask him to sit and talk. I am pleased that I did.

Whenever I talk to people about Brian, everyone says what a nice guy he is and how he is an incredible guitar player. I think that he is a good person, and I can say that he is also a great guitar player. He has a passion for music, and his head is on straight, as they say. He knows his strengths, weaknesses, and what he wants to do musically. I know he will be playing guitar and singing for as long as he wants to be a Solo Acoustic Musician.

You can learn even more about Brian on his website: brianleneschmidt.com

III. ABIGAIL RUDOLPH

Thursday, July 8th, 2021, 2 PM
Sea Sea Riders, Dunedin, FL.

As I arrived to meet Abigail Rudolph, I reflected that I had been looking forward to our conversation for a couple of weeks. She has a great enthusiasm for life, and has shared a genuine excitement with me about discussing the subject of being a SAM.

I have known Abigail for around ten years, and I enjoy her friendship. She has a beautiful smile and always seems to be happy. She also has a wonderful voice that I feel fortunate to hear when I can see her perform. We chose a place familiar to both of us to meet; it seemed fitting that it was one of the first places we had in common. We have played music in this restaurant for many years and are both extremely comfortable here.

Abigail is thirty years old, and started to play as a teenager — in her words, she first put a pick to the strings and strummed when she was fourteen. Her first experiences playing in front of people were at open mic nights. At that time, she only knew two songs. That same year, another local SAM was playing in a sports bar and invited her up to play her songs. She was quiet and shy, and the place was very loud. No one could hear her, so she was asked to play her songs again, and the audience quieted down to listen to her.

When she was beginning to play out professionally, she remembers that people would quiet down to hear her at her gigs. She admitted that at a certain point, she probably even took it for granted because it happened so often. It doesn't happen as often now. She added that she is even asked to turn down occasionally. For sixteen years, she has been playing guitar and singing. She has spent the last ten to eleven years consistently playing gigs for a living.

Abigail read my first book before our meeting, and I asked her if she found any information that jumped out at her. She said that she had never heard of the insurance I discussed. So we talked about having liability insurance coverage as a performer. I told her about the first time a venue manager asked me to have coverage and how it came as a surprise. She said it made sense to have coverage if something happened, like a customer tripping over her gear or a speaker falling over onto a customer. She also said she hoped that the venue would have insurance. I agree with her and think it is a good point to discuss with a venue, especially if they are the ones who bring up the topic of insurance.

She added that a lot of what she read in SAM1 were things that she had picked up along the way, and that she wished the book had existed when she started so she could have skipped ahead and not had to learn the hard way. She said that there were things in the book that she would not do, but that she could see the value of the information, and it's just not part of her setup or routine. I enjoyed hearing this because I told the first book from my perspective, and it was meant for people to use the information to find their own way of doing things.

We talked a bit about gear — she is currently playing a Taylor GS Mini guitar. She explained that she loved her Martin guitars for years, but when this Taylor model came out, she switched because it was lightweight and felt good to her. She suffered a car accident a while back, forcing her to adjust her gear, and the Taylor helps her avoid back pain at the end of a gig. She notices a difference in tone between the two brands but believes they both make quality instruments.

I asked her about her P.A. system, and she told me that she has been using QSC speakers and enjoying them for a while now. She typically uses two speakers, the K8 and K10 models, but is looking to add one or two more to her arsenal for outdoor gigs that may require a little more wattage and area coverage. She uses an old standby, the industry standard Shure microphone.

We began talking about our songbooks and our choices of songs to play. She feels it's important to learn songs that she likes and that she thinks people will enjoy. Finding songs that other local SAMs aren't playing around town is something else she focuses on. She admitted that she will sometimes learn a song for a fan who insists that she play it. Her sister kept after her to learn a specific song for a little while, until she relented and added it to her playlist. It wasn't something that she would have picked out initially, but she confessed that it had become a song that she likes performing.

We briefly talked about the "always buy two" rule I discussed in SAM1, and she agreed that it was a good rule to have in place. At least once, she had found herself running to the music store in the middle of a gig to buy a piece of gear when something didn't work, or she forgot something at home. She said she thinks it's good to go through that experience at least once. It helps us prepare for emergencies and plan how best we can avoid them.

Abigail is from the Tampa Bay area but spent about three and a half years living in Texas. Based on her descriptions of playing gigs there, I don't think it was a good fit for her. She told me that she was trying to play her original music, but the bars in her area were heavily focused on covers. She described an incredibly supportive music scene there, but that she came home to Florida, where she thinks she can play her original songs.

She said that sometimes a song hits you like lightning and flows right through you, while other times it takes years to complete an idea. She likes to think of it as a basket where she weaves in whatever musical hook she hears and then the words to it, doing it a little bit at a time. She added that sometimes she'll know what the chorus will be, and then write everything else around it, coming up with verses that match the vibe of the chorus. But other times, she will know the song's first line, and slowly construct the rest of the song. I liked her "weaving the basket" metaphor, and it makes sense given that you are crafting something a little bit at a time.

Abigail does play cover songs, but she always mixes original songs into her setlists. Also, she can play shows composed of only original songs. I know this part of Florida well, and she is right that venues here accept original music and encourage and foster a creative atmosphere. Every musician will have different experiences, and I am happy that she is back home here sharing her musical talents.

One difference between Abigail and me is that she tries not to play gigs on Sundays. This is a day that she sets aside for family time. Life requires balance, and everyone needs to find their way to live a fulfilling life. Reserving her Sundays for herself is part of making sure she has that kind of balance. She will accept a gig offer on a Sunday, but it is not a priority. Going kayaking or to the beach or hanging out with family takes precedence.

Abigail talked to me about the internal battle she fought with herself about doing this for a living. Becoming a full-time Solo Acoustic Musician was something that she researched while she was in college and just starting to play for money. She wanted this to be her only job, so she did an independent study, asking herself what it would take to make music her career. Could she make enough money per year to feel stable, happy, and not feel compromised? And would she not feel stressed out about it and not feel like it was a job? Because that could ruin it for her. When she was graduating college, the economy was awful, and she felt that if she didn't have a job, she would not be doing well. So she concluded that she would have to have a regular job alongside playing gigs.

At the time, she was taking any and every gig she could get. It didn't matter if someone was going to pay her fifty dollars to show up, set up her gear, and play for the night. She wanted to get as much experience as possible. She was doing opening sets and playing at a lot of open mics. So, she was going to school and doing all the gigs she could at the same time.

Now that she has found a balance that fits her lifestyle and a steady client list for her music, things have changed. When she looks at her calendar, she will evaluate things. Does she have enough family time? Is she playing too many shows back-to-back? She wants to have enough space between her gigs and not feel tired or worn out on stage. It wears down our batteries, and we need time to recharge. She thinks it's important to have energy every time she performs. She added that, she needs to be picky and choose which days she can work and when she needs to spend time recovering internally from all the noise and people that come with playing gigs.

I agreed and shared with her how I have discussed this aspect of being a performer many times. I have heard people say that ninety-five percent of people do not want to get up and talk in front of people. Whether that's a speech, a book report, or some kind of presentation, people in general will find it to be very stressful. I understand that as a SAM, I must find my alone time to balance out the time I spend in front of people performing. It takes guts to get up there on stage in front of everybody, whether for one song or three hours.

She said that she thinks there are common misconceptions about musicians. One example is that introverts are shy. Another one is that musicians are outgoing. Or that they are introverts or extroverts only. It's a mix. She explained that along her journey, she has concluded that as an artist, she can be a severe introvert or a shy introvert and still be a performing musician.

We discussed the pressure of being in front of a crowd and how it's like having a camera on you for a few hours. People watch and listen to every little thing you do while on stage. We both agree that it feels like most people don't seem to recognize that musicians go through this. I am always happy to have conversations with people who understand and go through the same things I do. There is comfort in knowing that I am not alone, and if I wanted to reach out and talk about being a performer, I could call a friend and share stories. We compared notes about getting nervous on stage and closing our eyes. She told me she remembers lyrics better with her eyes closed, and I responded that I would close my eyes sometimes when people stare at me. I think we both find comfort and a certain concentration level within ourselves when we play with our eyes closed.

I asked her how she gets her gigs. She responded that she is lucky to be at the point where word-of-mouth and references are keeping her calendar full enough for her. She recalled bringing her CD or press pack to various venues when she first started her SAM journey, though. She would also go to open mics to audition for the venue hosting the events. She added that nothing could prove your concept better than seeing you perform in person.

At this point, Abigail is not looking to gig every day and is more laid-back about chasing down gigs. She explains that when she gets into a new venue now, it mostly happens because she is covering for someone else, and the management likes her. Then she can book herself there and continue to play at the venue. She finds it more about networking than going door-to-door or from one venue to another giving a sales pitch. If she and her husband go out for dinner, and the restaurant has live music, she will look for a way to have a conversation with an employee about the fact that she is a musician.

I like that Abigail believes that she is truly fortunate to have so many word-of-mouth references, and I know from experience that it is nice to have someone reach out to you because someone else suggested you. She talked about how she was so young when she started that she had help from friends to get gigs. She continued by saying that it shows that you should be friendly to other musicians in your musical community or circle, because you never know when that could help you get a gig.

We segued into talking about promotion, and Abigail revealed that she posts her gigs on a website called ReverbNation. This allows her to only post once, because the site will share her gig dates and times on other social media platforms for her. When she books a gig, she puts it on her ReverbNation page's calendar, and it will auto-post on other sites two days before her gig. I did not know about this, and I must admit that I thought it was pretty cool. She also keeps a paper calendar and one on her phone. It is always good to have a backup in case something happens to one of the other calendars.

Since she had read SAM1, I asked her about her load-ins and load-outs. She liked my "dummy check" idea and said she always says, "check twice." She recalled a few times when she had left something like her fan behind at a gig. I told her I had almost left my chair behind recently, but the dummy check saved me.

Pro Tip: *Tip your bartenders. Even if it's a few dollars and they just got you water. Even if your drinks and food are complimentary, tip them a few one-dollar bills or a five every time you play there, and they will be happier about you playing there.*

We talked about working the crowd. She says that her number one thing to do on stage is to be relatable. Just be yourself. Don't try to be an icon that you are not. Just be as close to your offstage self as possible because the more you try to put on an act to be this other thing, the harder it is to keep up that character. Abigail stays as authentic as possible. She says that she will laugh at herself in the microphone when she messes up. Because what else is she going to do? Act freaked out that she made a mistake, while everybody else is wondering what's going on? So, her advice is to be real.

There will be crowds you can't win over. Maybe you are not the right fit for the venue, and you have to recognize that that's ok. You're not a bad musician, it's just not the right stage for you. Abigail told me that she played a New Year's Eve gig when she was a brand-new folk/indie artist. She had learned new songs for the gig. When she got up on the stage, she tried to be as loud and upbeat as possible because it was New Year's Eve. She was cut an hour early, with pay for the entire night.

The employees felt bad because the owner loved her music. But the crowd and the bartenders and staff working that night instantly realized that she was not a good fit for New Year's Eve. Abigail knew it, too. She recalled asking the owner, "Are you sure about booking me for that night? I'm indie-folk, quiet, and little, and it's a minimal sound. I'm not a party band." They asked her to play anyway. The owner insisted. She recalled, "It was one of those nothing-against-me/I-didn't-do-anything-wrong situations." She had been playing at the venue next door regularly, and both places were owned by the same person. So it wasn't like they hated her. It just wasn't a good fit for New Year's Eve.

I know the place she was talking about, and it's a three-part business. One part restaurant, one part lounge/bar, and one part nightclub. She was an excellent fit for the lounge but not the nightclub, especially for a night like New Year's Eve, when people want to have a loud party.

Abigail explained that when the crowd is not into what she is doing on a regular night (which happens to all of us), she thinks of it as free practice. She's getting paid to practice. So, if no one is paying attention anyway, she might try some songs that she doesn't usually play. If she messes up, she messes up. She won't be as critical of herself.

If she treats the situation like a paid rehearsal, she can still make the time productive and still enjoy herself. I understood what she was saying, and have done the same thing in the past. Some audiences just don't care and would probably prefer us not even be there. We continued talking about playing different genres and switching styles to engage the crowd. After spending a lot of time trying to please audiences and failing, sometimes we have to play a few songs for ourselves.

I asked her if she had any go-to songs that she could turn a crowd around and get a positive response. She said that "500 Miles" by the Proclaimers will usually work for her, and get people singing along. I have to agree that it is a very catchy song. She added that "Ooh La La" by the Faces is another go-to crowd-pleaser that can change a gig immediately. Lastly, she says that when she plays Bobby McFerrin's "Don't Worry, Be Happy," it usually changes the audience's attitude to one of happiness, getting them more into what she is doing.

We discussed what happens if even these songs don't work to flip the crowd in our favor, and we found ourselves back at the paid rehearsal solution. It's disheartening when I have given my all to please the audience and can't seem to break through to them. After that, I can start to want to do songs for myself or try new things that I am not familiar with yet. As Abigail put it, "Let's just make the best of an unpleasant situation." She continued, "Sometimes it's ironic because on one of those nights, you can make the best tips of your life. People might come up at the end of the night and throw lots of money into the tip jar." Recently, she had a night like that, where at the end of the gig, she made lots of tips, was offered a wedding gig, and was told by the venue owner that she was his new favorite act. All of this after a night of zero response from the audience, making her think they didn't like her.

As we talked about the weather on gigs, we mulled over the same old policies. The stuff we do to protect our gear and to communicate with venue owners or managers. Abigail lit up because she remembered playing at an event where the weather was not so lovely. The concert was in downtown Clearwater, and was hosted by one of the local restaurants. The street was blocked off, making it kind of a festival atmosphere. The owner was supplying a stage and a soundman for multiple acts, making it a plug-and-play situation: she wouldn't have to set up her own P.A. Abigail was on stage, in the middle of her second song, when a massive windy storm dumped rain all over the area. There were two tents on the stage, and they filled up with water extremely fast and didn't hold. They released the water between them, directly onto the main mixing board of the sound system. More than five thousand dollars' worth of gear — ruined.

As this happened, musicians grabbed their gear, and people crammed into bars and restaurants lining the street, including the host restaurant, all laughing about getting out of the storm. Abigail saw the sound guy wheeling in his equipment at the back entrance of the bar and that he had gone from a happy sound guy to a water-soaked mess in minutes. Abigail felt horrible for the guy. She talked to the venue owner and decided to forgo her own pay and donate it to the sound guy to help with his gear expenses. It can take years to build up the amount of equipment he was using that day, and weather can ruin it in an instant. To me, that is scary stuff. She always remembers this story when someone asks her to set up outside, and it might rain that day. She tells them she watched someone lose all their gear to a storm. It's not worth the risk for one gig. She adds that stories like this are why she always gets the extra two-year insurance or warranty on equipment when she buys things like speakers.

I asked her about her protocol for arriving at a gig. How early does she get to the venue? She told me that she likes to be there an hour before the show starts. Being on time or even a little early is super important if it's her first time at a new spot. She might even go an hour and a half early for a first gig at a new venue. We both agreed that going from a regular guitar case to a backpack case is an upgrade because of the load-in. Filling the extra space in the backpack with a songbook, iPad or other accessories is another advantage.

If you don't already have one, Abigail says, "Get a power strip!" She called it a huge life hack. Having that surge protector could save your gear. She said that it's not just in case lightning hits the building. If someone turns on a vacuum and causes a breaker to pop and shuts off the power unexpectedly, it could damage your equipment. She has had a mixer destroyed before by this very scenario. Losing gear to a power surge would make anyone regret not having one plugged in to protect their equipment. We discussed the newly upgraded versions with USB power outlets. This can help protect an iPad or cell phone from a power surge.

Pro Tip: *Buy and use a power strip surge protector for all your equipment.* — *Abigail Rudolph*

I asked her if she has any unique or fun accessories, and Abigail told me that she has a keychain pick holder. It has saved her many times because we SAMs lose guitar picks all the time. It's a small triangle that she can put picks in, and then she always has one just in case. It is small and holds four or five picks. She told me that she has a label maker and uses it to label her equipment. She puts a label near one end of each of her cables, and sticks one with her name across the bottom of her speakers. She does this to protect herself if she accidentally leaves something behind when loading out, and to help identify her gear if someone steals something. Almost all of her equipment has a label somewhere on it. I haven't done this myself, but I love the idea, and I might be doing it soon. She says that musicians can also use it in a band or recording setting if someone wants to label cables for specific use like Bass, Keyboard, Vocal, Drums (which could have individual use cables), Guitar, etc.

When alcohol is available on a gig, her basic rule for health and nutrition is to go one for one. If she has a drink, then she has a glass of water. She said this helps her not strain her voice by drying out her throat. Also, she pointed out that you are not getting inebriated because the water helps balance the alcohol intake. The point is to maintain control and not be drunk on stage. Also, to be able to drive home safely. So if you do have an alcoholic drink during a gig, make sure that you have plenty of water.

We had to reschedule our interview because Abigail wasn't feeling good on the original date. She had to cancel gigs and stay home. So we talked about resting our voices. When Abigail got back to gigging after a week off, she pointed out that she would choose minimal impact songs, and knowing what she had in her songbook helped. Singing a lower harmony note is a solution she offered. No one will notice, and it will still sound good. Another tip she added would be not to try to impress people when you don't feel strong about your vocals. I think I understand. While you can still sing in key and sound good, sometimes you might have to skip an exceptionally high note or big note that you sing. It's about choosing to sound good instead of strained. You can always impress people next time.

Part of taking care of ourselves is trying to live a healthy lifestyle. This can be a challenge when navigating the bar scene for a living, but it's not impossible. Abigail brought up the stereotypes that people attach to being a musician. I was surprised to hear that she deals with these because I have a good idea of the kind of person she is in real life. But evidently, people have assumed that Abigail is a drug addict or a stoner, that she is lazy, and that being a musician isn't a real job. She gets up at 7 AM every day, and takes her choice to be a working musician very seriously. She puts effort and thought into what she is doing. She tells people, "This is all I do, and I love it." (Picture a big smile.)

When it comes to tip cans and merchandise displays, Abigail again used the word "authenticity" and said to be yourself. If you can get away with a paint can with stickers on it, and it fits your vibe, then that's what you should do. If you're the flowery and artsy type, reflect that in your display. Make it a part of your show. She considers this to be another chance for self-expression. She explained that she has seen people write a joke on their tip can sign, which may be part of their identity. She told me about another one she has seen: a gimmick involving two tip cans, one for each of the two sports teams on the TV. I told her I had never seen this before and that it was genius. You could trade the team names or logos for any opposing opinions. Left-handed or Right-handed. Up or Down. Hot or Cold. Beer or Wine. I think you get the idea. (I don't suggest using political parties or religious affiliations, because that could cause fights.) I think it's a creative way to engage the crowd and potentially drive your totals up.

Abigail brought up playing gigs at nursing homes and piqued my interest at once. I have never done this type of gig before. Her first word to describe this type of gig was "magical." She said, "This is a good fit for me because I like to play all the oldies. Like Elvis and songs like 'Stand By Me.' Like really sweet Fifties and Sixties songs." She described the feeling of playing in a nursing home full of Alzheimer's patients, who are all in their seventies or eighties, as like lighting a match. It is the music of their youth, and they react and come alive.

---

*Music imprints itself in the brain deeper than
any other human experience. Music brings back
the feeling of life when nothing else can.*
— Dr. Oliver Sacks

Their eyes light up, singing all the songs word for word. The people who work there will tell you that the patients may not even know what they just ate for lunch. But then they are singing with you on a song from their youth that they haven't heard in a long time. Abigail said, "It's powerful. It's meaningful. It's an amazing feeling." I think it is beautiful how music can be a memory trigger. When the people light up in response to the music she plays, it is something she feels in her body too. It is the opposite of the situation we discussed earlier, where we could be playing in a bar, and no one seems to care. In this situation, not only do the people care, but they also light up with joy! We as musicians feel that joy, and it becomes a shared experience of happiness with the audience. That is a truly remarkable and magical thing. Seeing someone who was emotionless just minutes before changing into a smiling happy person is fantastic. When this happens, it fulfills part of the purpose of being able to share music with others.

One of her policies since the beginning has been to accept as many invites to play charity events as she can. She will also donate her time to play music for a celebration of life. She said, "It's an honor to be chosen and trusted with providing the music. It's a significant part of their day. Music can be so healing and powerful." Abigail explained that her heart feels good when she does it because she is giving of herself. As I pointed out in SAM1, I think it is essential to use our musical talents for good and help people. Abigail agrees and does the same things in her musical life.

Abigail's future will include writing and recording new songs, continuing to play gigs, and following her dream of being a musician for a living. She has been writing new songs and has been feeling inspired lately. Her energy is up, and she wants to record the new songs she has written during the last year. She thinks about her future family and having children while balancing her musical lifestyle. She is surrounded by family and friends who will enjoy this chapter of her life and support her future endeavors.

Abigail stated that her brand is firmly one of integrity and is family friendly. She is one of my top five go-to phone calls when looking for someone to cover a gig for me. She has proven to be dependable in all the ways anyone would ask of someone they recommend. I look forward to hearing the new songs she has written and seeing where she goes with her musical journey. Having friends like her in my musical community is important to me. I hope all of you find a special someone like her in your musical life.

After a couple of hours had gone by, we realized we had to move on with our day. It was so easy to talk with her and hang out that I think we could have sat there for quite a while longer. When I thought about doing these interviews, I hoped they would be fun, and that I would learn more about some of my friends. That was what happened with Abigail Rudolph. I enjoyed spending time with an old friend and talking about being a Solo Acoustic Musician.

IV. MARK HANSON

Monday, July 19th, 2021, 2 PM
BRGR Kitchen & Bar, Treasure Island Beach Resort, Treasure Island, FL

I arrived at Mark's house right before 2 PM. I met him many years ago when we both played at a restaurant in Madeira Beach that had an afternoon act and an evening act. We connected one day when one of us was packing up and the other was loading in. But after all these years, we had never hung out together, and I had never been to his house.

He lives in a neighborhood in the north part of St. Petersburg, not far from the beach. So after showing me some guitars and gear in his music room, we headed to the resort to grab some burgers, coffee, and a great view of the Gulf of Mexico. It was over ninety degrees, but we were seated at a table in the shade on the pool deck, where we were blessed with a slight breeze. I love the beach, and the hotel wasn't busy on a Monday afternoon, so it was an excellent environment to relax and share time talking about SAM life.

Mark pointed out that there weren't people to give us advice when we started playing gigs. We had no one to ask questions like "What if this happens?", "How do I do this?", etc. Now mind you, he has twenty years on me, but we agree about this. He added that there are times when you must come up with something to get you through the night, when something isn't going right on a gig. He recalled a friend calling him in a panic, saying, "Mark, you gotta help me."

He replied, "Whaddya need?"

His friend said, "I blew my voice out, and I've got a gig tonight. What am I going to do?"

Mark responded, "Well, this is how you get through it. One, drink just ridiculous amounts of water all day long. You want to keep flushing whatever's in your throat and your sinuses out. Just get it so it can move. Secondly, how much do you weigh?"

The guy said, "One hundred and sixty-five pounds."

Mark said, "Take three ibuprofen one hour before the gig. You want to reduce and minimize inflammation as you go along. Three, do not talk to anyone before the gig and do not talk to anyone on your breaks. You have trained yourself to sing, but you have not trained yourself to talk, and there's a big difference. I've seen more guys blow their voices out talking on breaks than singing for four hours."

At this point I interjected, saying, "Especially if it's loud in the room."

Mark replied, "Of course. And if you're hyped up, maybe you're nervous; you're going a million miles an hour." He continued, "Now. Water. Ibuprofen. Don't talk. Here's what will get you through the gig. You will find out very quickly what you have access to vocally and what you don't. When you're coming up to a passage that you can't pull off, it will not happen." He said emphatically, "Catch someone's eye and laugh. No one expects you to hit a note while laughing."

Pro Tip: *When you are not feeling vocally strong, and a big note that is hard to sing is coming up, catch a fit of laughter.* —Mark Hanson

---

Three and a half minutes into our conversation, I already felt like I had absorbed a lifetime of knowledge just being in Mark's presence. Something about his manner and the words he said let me know that he had been doing this forever. He wore comfortable shoes, khaki pants, and a Hawaiian shirt, and had a tan and the laid-back personality that I expected of a veteran of the beach musician scene.

He knows his stuff for sure. He is more technical than I am about gear and guitars. He knows all the specifics about his equipment. I envy people like him who know all the little details about everything. I have never been that way regarding model numbers and specifications.

I had never heard of doing the laughing thing Mark recommends when I was not feeling strong about my vocals, but it made me smile and think about trying it the next time I have a rough day vocally.

Mark told me about a time when he had blown out his voice. He was doing a two-gig day out in direct sunlight. At his gig the next day, he had to start singing at 1 PM, at a venue that was a 90-minute drive from home. So he had to leave at 10:30 AM to load in and set up at noon. He remembered getting to bed at 3:30 AM. As he told me this story, I was doing math in my head, and I knew that he was not getting enough rest for his voice to recover. When he woke up, he couldn't even make a sound. He took a hot shower, gargled water, and waited at least half an hour before even trying to make a low hum with his vocal cords. He did this just to get a vibration going. While setting up his gear, he tried to hum and open his vocal range. He recalls having a half an octave of range and was hoping to open more if he could. He had no bottom range and no top range to his voice. Even having anything barely in the middle, he had to play the whole gig.

This was at a large outdoor summer venue, a big resort, and it paid $275 for the afternoon shift. That's a good-paying gig now, so it was a great-paying gig 18 years ago. Mark did not want to cancel and was going to do everything he could to get through the gig. At the end of the show, the manager who brought him his check said, "Good job today." Mark rumbled something inaudible. The guy asked, "Are you OK?"

Mark replied, "No. I blew my voice out last night. I can barely talk right now." The manager remarked that he had heard Mark had lost his voice, and was shocked because he'd looked like he was having so much fun. (Mark had been "laughing" a lot that day...)

Mark is currently sixty-seven years old and started playing guitar around nine. The first time he played in public was in seventh grade, at around twelve years old. His first guitar had nylon strings, and the first song he learned was "Teenager In Love." His friend who lived up the street had an older brother who had started playing guitar but then gave it up. The older brother had a songbook in which his instructor had written out the words and chords to several songs. Mark inherited this songbook. We had a good chuckle after singing a part of the song together. It's an old-school tune from way back.

Mark played in bands until about forty years ago, when he started doing solo gigs. Around 1983 he became a full-time Solo Acoustic Musician. He was living in New Jersey then, near the Pennsylvania border. He remembers that the transition from a band to being a solo performer was weird. He was used to the dynamics of how the band could control a room. He says that a solo act can't do it the same way. Of course, he has figured it out over the years and adapted to working the crowd as a SAM.

I pointed out that the restaurant where we were talking didn't have music, which triggered a conversation about where they might put a musician. We were covered by a roof and out of the direct sunlight, and there was a large pool area between us and the beach, with the usual pool fence blocking it off. There was no tiki bar outside, and the wait staff tended to guests by the pool. We didn't ever settle on a good place for a musician to set up. It was a toss-up between being covered and far away from people, or being out from under the roof and closer to everyone.

Mark does play another hotel right up the street, and has been doing that gig every Friday for years. I cringed a little as he described the roof above the stage at that venue. It didn't sound too good to me. The stage didn't have side flaps either. After years of being beaten down by the weather, it sounded like it needed repairs.

The head bartender there knows that Mark is the type of person who would throw tarps over everything and wait half an hour if he had proper protection. He could take the tarps off, turn everything back on, and start playing again once the weather improves. Because the people will scatter, and the place will clear out as the storm passes over. But they'll come back out, and the bar will be jumping again when it's gone. This contingency plan is not possible, though, because of the stage layout, and the head bartender, who pays him, knows this. So as soon as it starts to drizzle, Mark shuts off the power and packs up. Then he is paid his total fee for the gig. They are very understanding of the situation, and they love Mark there. I was happy to hear that they take care of him like this. The head bartender has been there for seventeen years, and he is quick to make sure that the musicians get a full day's pay if they are on time and set up to play. Maybe they have played a half hour, or perhaps they are in their second set. He still pays them for the entire gig if the rain stops them. I was delighted to hear this because although it should be standard practice, not every venue treats its musicians this way.

Mark told me that he knows two musicians who quit playing gigs because of only receiving half pay in a situation like this. They were on time, set up, played music for an hour, and then it rained on them. After this, they were given half pay and had to go home, unload the vehicle, bring everything inside, dry it all off, make sure their equipment still worked, and deal with the stress of the whole situation.

Some venues don't realize we are doing more work, not less, when dealing with lousy weather. To then only get half pay is horrible for the musician. These guys said that it was just not worth it. I felt terrible for them and said that I thought it was the venue's responsibility to provide us with a safe place to play. I know Mark is grateful for being treated with respect by his Friday spot, and that's probably one of the many reasons he has been there for so long.

Mark remembered another place that he used to play that managed the weather and pay situation very well. This beach hotel tiki bar doesn't have live music anymore but what they used to do was this: If they didn't call you to cancel because of the weather and you showed up on time, ready to load in and set up, you got half pay. The moment you showed up, it was a half-paid gig. If you played one song, it was a full-pay gig. Of course, if you set up and during or immediately after your first song a storm hit, you would be paid in full for the gig. The main reason for this policy was that the guy in charge of booking the entertainment was a retired agent.

We also talked about double bookings. As I do, Mark has musician friends, and he said that two of them were talking a few days before about showing up to a gig and being double-booked. Mark tells me that he has had more than one manager admit that they messed up. But whose pocket does the money come out of when this happens? The answer is that the musician who doesn't get to play that day loses money. Even though it's the manager who messed up, it will cost a musician money. How is that even remotely OK?

Booking gigs is a big part of the Solo Acoustic Musician lifestyle. It's an ongoing and never-ending campaign. Mark has been a SAM for a long time, and this is what he said to me about booking: "Well, so much of it is having energy and emotional strength to go out and put yourself in front of these people. It got to me in the last two or three years. You walk in, and you know that as soon as that manager sees you, he goes, 'Oh, crap.'" I took him to mean that the manager was tired of musicians approaching him. The people in charge of the calendar at venues are often overrun by musicians pitching their sales materials.

When Mark first moved to the area, he got booked up relatively quickly. He says that there were no surprises and that he knew before moving down here what the level of musicianship would be in the area. He tells me that he estimated that it would take him three months to have a full schedule.

Finding places that will book you instantly does happen, but Mark questions why they have openings. He says that they probably screw things up. Most places will have their calendar taken care of for at least a few months in advance. The fact that a venue has openings for immediate bookings could indicate that they oversee their calendar unprofessionally. He said that none of that was a surprise when he got to

Florida. But he had the energy and the nerve to go knocking on doors for four or five hours a day to check out every place he could find.

As he put it, he had a formula. "If I drop off this number of CDs, and this amount of people will listen to it, I will be able to get this number of gigs out of it. Out of every ten gigs I get through soliciting like this, one or two of them will become long-term. That could be once or twice a month. Certain other gigs will be one-and-done."

When Mark is on a gig, he drinks club soda with lemon. He says, "It's water with carbonation and citric acid from the lemon, and it clears all the stuff out of your throat."

Mark enjoys writing songs and even sang a few a cappella for me during our time together. I will be honest and say that I don't know how he remembers all those lyrics. He writes funny songs, which I think is a remarkable ability to have. Writing any kind of song is challenging, but writing funny songs is another level of talent. The "Mark Hanson songwriting method" is to avoid it at all costs if he can. That was what he told me when I asked him if he had a process for writing songs. I was laughing as he explained what he meant.

A film music composer in L.A. that Mark works with sends him projects. He writes the lyrics for them, and he will get twenty of these projects at a time. The mock-ups for these songs always come in big batches like this. On top of the number of songs that he may be sent, they come with strict deadlines. Sometimes, Mark completes a song, and then it's never used, only to be recycled back to him for all new lyrics using the same melody. I was getting a little stressed out just listening to him tell me about it, so I can only imagine having to be on the clock, creatively, like that.

Mark also told me about the emphasis on the exactness of the notes and that he cannot adjust the melodies. He has to write lyrics within the parameters set by the composer. It's just another aspect of the songwriting process that he must go through when working with this person. It's very different from having the freedom to write songs any old way that I want to. Mark gets profoundly serious and into a song, so much that he could be thinking about it for weeks. Have you ever been humming a song you heard on the radio all day? Mark is doing that while writing lyrics to an already prepared melody. It would seem like an obsession to someone else, but to Mark, it is just part of his process.

Mark told me that he tends to start working around 1 AM. He said that there is nothing good on TV then and no one is calling him, so there are no distractions. He had all these pedals left over from the late Seventies and early Eighties, like original BOSS chorus pedals. All of them crackle. But he knew that you could go in with ultra-fine sandpaper, make it into a cone, and scrape all the crud out. Then you hit it with DeoxIT. Then you're good to go.

(DeoxIT is a spray that is a fast-acting deoxidizing solution designed for use as a general treatment for connectors, contacts, and other metal surfaces. More than a contact cleaner, DeoxIT chemically improves electrical connections.)

Mark has a music room in his house where he has equipment set up. But he also has a guitar repair workbench, and it's there that he has all of his tools. He told me that he gets his pedals as clean as if they were brand new. So now it's two in the morning, and he thought he could make a cool pedalboard with these pedals if he only had some wood. He said that he was working on the project for the next two weeks, and then he started to sing an a cappella song for me right there at the table. It was a funny, adult content song that he wrote using the words "If I only had some wood" as his inspiration. The song didn't have any profanity, but it was full of innuendos in the lyrical content. He told me that he rarely sings this song, and it's usually at an open mic in a place where he doesn't want to get a gig. At first, I thought he was telling me a story about gear and how he cleans old guitar pedals. But it ended up being a story about songwriting, which is what we were talking about in the first place.

Mark has a fun thing he does with a bartender that he has worked with for years. They have been at this for a long time, and if you read this and want to try it for yourself at a gig, you might want to discuss it with your bartender before you go on stage. Whenever Mark wants a club soda, he sings "Happy Birthday" to the bartender, and says loudly into the microphone, "That's right, it's your bartender's birthday! I hope you brought presents."

My eyebrows perked up, and I said, "I bet they tip him better."

Mark nodded, indicating that the audience responded positively. "Oh yeah, he comes over with a ten-dollar bill in one hand and my drink in the other and leans over to me to say, 'That never gets old.'" From a working SAM's point of view, this is genius. Mark is thirsty. He gets the crowd to sing along with him while at the same time sending a secret message to the bartender. The bartender is tipped more and is happy. Mark gets his drink. Mark joked that when he sings "Happy Birthday" to someone else in the audience, it's almost like Pavlov's bells signaling the bartender to make him a drink.

After I've been on a gig at a particular venue for a long time, I know that I must keep it fresh for myself, the employees, and the audience. Mark says that he will tell the bartender to let him know if the staff get sick of a song he has been playing. If that's the case, he says he won't play that song at that venue for years. He has hundreds of songs to choose from and doesn't want to keep repeating songs that are becoming annoying for the employees to listen to again. Over the years, Mark has built up an extensive catalog of songs to choose from, and he is still learning songs to keep his music list fresh.

When he is working the crowd at a gig and reading the audience, he looks at their ages and thinks about what time of year it is. We have different tourist seasons here in Florida, and Mark has been playing on the beach for a long time. The time of year can influence his song choices, based on who is visiting. I asked him to tell me his response to the age-old question from an audience member who wanted to know what kind of music you play. As working SAMs, we have been asked this question many times, and I wanted to know what he says to people when they ask him, "What kind of music do you play?"

He says that he plays Seventies and early Eighties pop, and classic country. This is how most of us respond, by settling on an era and genre. But Mark takes it to another level when he reaches down to pick up what he calls his "Song Menu" and hands it to an audience member. He tells them, "Here is my song menu. Pick out whatever song you want, and I'll cook it up for you." He keeps these printed song menus in a folder next to his tip jar on his merchandise table. A little sign on the folder says, "Pick a song, and I'll cook it up."

This is another highly creative way a SAM makes the merchandise and tip table something unique that fits their personality. When someone comes up to him to make a request, he can control the situation by directing them to order a song from the menu. All too often, I am confronted by a person asking for a bunch of different songs that I don't know how to play. This concept ends the awkward back-and-forth, yes-or-no question-and-answer session between an audience member and a SAM.

Pro Tip: *Keep business cards in your tip can.*
People can get to them easily, and the wind won't
blow them away when you're playing outside.

I heard a new perspective from Mark when I asked him about engaging the audience. He tells me that it can be hard to get the attention of a table with three different couples. When six people are seated at the same table and are having conversations with each other, they haven't heard all of each other's stories yet. But a two-top (a table with two people) can be easier to engage, especially if it's a married couple in their forties or older, because they have already heard each other's life stories. The two-top is looking for a new experience or a distraction from their everyday lives. As a SAM, we can engage and entertain them. He adds that if you can get them to play along, someone at the six-top will notice and want to join in the fun.

Mark actively looks for opportunities to engage the crowd. He is seeking someone who wants to be entertained. He likes to have an enjoyable time and create an atmosphere of fun when he plays a gig. Even if there are only thirty minutes left, he will look for someone in the crowd to engage. He doesn't want to regret not taking the chance and reaching out to people in the audience. This was a lesson, even for me, to stay alert and present in the moment. I understand that it can be harder to exude that positive energy towards the end of a gig when I am tired and ready to go home. But this can be the exact moment when the opportunity to reach someone in the audience will present itself. I know I will remember this thought for a long time. In the future, I am sure I will be nearing the end of a gig and find myself feeling tired. Then I will remember Mark's voice, and I will scan the crowd for someone to talk to about what they want to hear.

He said to keep your mind, heart, and eyes open. If an opportunity appears, take advantage of it. He says that the only time he has ever been upset with himself after a gig was while driving home and realizing that he saw an opportunity and was too lazy to act on it. This upsets him, and it doesn't happen very often. He feels that it is a betrayal of who he is, and I think I can relate to that. He says, "I'm not there to finish up four hours and get out. I'm not here to look at my watch for four hours. I'm there to try to entertain and to make a connection." He admitted that we all do it, though. We get tired, have three more songs, and will be done for the night. I agree and think that all we can do is try to be better each time we take the stage. Mark added that anytime someone starts to talk to you, they give you an opportunity.

He says he has developed certain things to say after specific songs that engage the crowd. These can develop into routines. One example of this was him saying, "Just checking for hippies," at the end of a Grateful Dead song. I laughed when he said this; I think humor is a great way to engage the audience and make people smile. I told Mark that I like it when I see live music and the act does something like what he just described. I don't care for it much when a SAM just stands there playing songs and doesn't try to engage the audience.

I know it can be tough to do, and it is a skill that takes time to develop, but as a person trying to entertain, I have to try.

Mark explained that non-verbal cues are happening all the time through body language. The way we stand or sit onstage can make us more or less approachable. As Solo Acoustic Musicians, we have to be aware of this. We could be turning people off to us without realizing it. Mark told me that there are musicians who give off a "leave me alone" vibe because they are afraid of interaction.

In SAM1, I talked about how smiling can change a gig for the better. Mark told me about a musician he knows who is a rather good guitar player, but he noticed that the man went right from one song to the next one very quickly. Mark concluded that the guy only had so many songs and didn't want to take any requests. So he made sure that the people didn't have any time between songs to talk to him. Mark prefers to take a minute or two between songs so that people can speak to him. He tells me that he could quickly start right into another song, but he likes people to know they can make requests. I agree with him about this, because I do the same thing.

Mark made me laugh for about twenty minutes with the little one-liners and routines he has developed over the years. I don't have enough pages in this book for all of his jokes and stories.

We moved onto the topic of gear, and Mark tells me that he plays a D'Angelico guitar that he's customized. Remember I told you he has a workbench and is truly knowledgeable about his gear. Mark is using Elixir Polyweb 10-gauge strings. He sings through a SHURE Beta 57 microphone and uses an Alesis SR18 drum machine and a looper pedal to create some of his songs. By using the SR18 in pattern mode, he can use the two separate foot pedals to control the patterns he is doing in real time. He also uses a volume control foot pedal to fade in and out. He also has a vocal harmonizer in his toolbox. Currently, Mark uses powered JBL speakers. He likes the versatility of powered speakers because if he needs more power, he can add one.

After we ate our burgers, we chatted about other aspects of our local scene. It was fun to hear Mark's stories and perspectives on things that we have in common. When we left the resort, we talked some more as I drove us back to his house. Mark has a wealth of stories and a remarkable memory for all the little details. I think he could probably write his own book about all the things he has seen and done. I knew I had only scratched the surface of his wisdom and knowledge in the couple of hours we spent together. He is a genuinely nice person, and it was fun getting to know him better. I had a wonderful time hanging out on the beach and listening to him tell me stories about his life as a Solo Acoustic Musician. Check out his website and listen to a few songs.

markhanson.com

V. CHASE HARVEY

Tuesday, July 20th, 2021, 2 PM
Barfly, Safety Harbor, FL

You've probably noticed a pattern here, with me meeting everyone for interviews at 2 PM on weekdays. I think it has to do with the fact that we are all working SAMs, booked on the weekends. Also, the places we met had busy lunch and dinner crowds, and I tried to get in during quieter midafternoon stretches.

I have known Chase for about ten years, and we spoke on his twenty-eighth birthday. I remember when he was younger and just starting to become a SAM. The first times I remember hearing him play were at an open mic that I hosted. I may have even been one of his mentors. He went to other open mics and made friends with other musicians on the scene. He was not shy about asking for information or guidance to learn about booking or playing gigs. I never influenced his music, but I did have conversations with him about the business side of things.

Chase has always been a Florida boy, born and raised, who wanted to play chill music by the beach. Surfing and skateboarding were part of his identity, and they're also a part of his musical lifestyle—he takes a laid-back approach to playing and singing relaxing music.

We met at a place where we have both performed for years. As I pulled into the parking lot, I remembered seeing Chase loading in his speakers on a skateboard years earlier. I made a mental note to ask him about it.

Typically, when either of us is at this venue, we are always inside by the stage and the bar. So today, I suggested that we grab a high-top table out on the front porch to have a different perspective. People would be walking by, cars would be driving by, and we would be talking about our lives as Solo Acoustic Musicians. I ordered him a birthday margarita and we started talking.

For Chase, it all started when his dad began learning how to play guitar, while he was stationed in Korea. His father was in the Air Force, and would have been in his early twenties. His father didn't play much guitar for a long time as he settled down to raise a family. When Chase was ten, they went to the house of one of his father's friends. That guy sat down and started playing guitar, and Chase thought it was the coolest thing. It was the first time anyone had played in front of him in his life, to his memory. The guy also sang along to songs for the small group of about ten friends. It was like a private home concert.

Chase enjoyed the music and thought it was cool. His dad told him that he played guitar as well, and bought one from a pawn shop the next day. There had never been a guitar in the house until that point. His father started out playing songs by James Taylor. Chase recalls that his dad was a decent picker, but mostly played with his fingers. These days Chase does both. He uses a pick and plays fingerstyle, because his father did.

Chase remembers sitting with a heavy Washburn guitar on his lap, trying to hit notes. His dad taught him to play Deep Purple's "Smoke On the Water," and Chase would use his thumb to hit the notes. This became something fun for him to do as a hobby.

His older sister and his cousin were learning how to play at the same time, and they would teach him as well. He says that it was always something fun to do but he didn't take it seriously. When he was around twelve, he focused on playing chords and learning to sing songs. He was beginning to be able to sing and play simultaneously. Over the next couple of years, he began to play barre chords. We both remembered that barre chords hurt our hands when we were that young. They can be discouraging initially, but obviously, we pushed on.

He says that he didn't want to be a great guitar player. He just really enjoyed doing it. He had an old classical guitar, which he said was easier to play barre chords on. Pressing down the nylon strings is not as harsh for a beginner as the steel strings on an acoustic guitar. Chase said, "It was a slow burn for me. It was just something that I would do after a soccer game. Sports were always number one for me. So, when I would get home from a soccer game and sit down while watching TV, I would just strum certain things. Whatever sounded good to me. Write down songs for no reason."

During high school, Chase was still focused on sports, but he played guitar for his friends. They encouraged him, and they would compliment him on his abilities.

But he always loved listening to music. So he and his dad would go together every Wednesday to see a local musician that they liked. This was about fourteen years ago, when Chase was fourteen, and I knew who he was talking about and where the guy would have been playing. I moved here fourteen years ago, and that guy was one of the first other musicians I found. I also liked to go to the same place to see him play. Maybe Chase and I were in the same room and didn't know each other yet.

Chase recalled, "It was fun to watch him because of how simple his setup was." He noticed this because as a teenager he was overwhelmed by the amount of gear some people used. Chase felt like he was the least technical guy regarding equipment. He would see other musicians with stuff like laptops for backing tracks and lots of speakers. Everybody on the beach played Jimmy Buffett songs with steel drums in the background and things like that. It seemed strange to Chase; he just wanted to play guitar and sing. The guy we talked about didn't use tracks or have a loop pedal. He had a basic, minimalist approach, and Chase thought that was impressive. Unbelievably, that same guy still uses the same guitar, powered mixer, and the same speaker set up today.

Chase didn't use a loop pedal either at first, but now he has embraced it. He tells me that it's great when he can play music and save his voice by not having to sing the whole night. When Chase is gigging four to six nights a week, he can't afford to sing every minute. He says he probably sings thirty or forty minutes less per gig using the loop pedal. It has also had the side effect of helping him become a better guitar player. Now he also incorporates a drum pad into his setup. This extra gear gives him the freedom to challenge himself musically and share his musical expression.

It wasn't until Chase was eighteen or nineteen that he started going to some open mics. The reality of playing gigs for money started to happen for him when he was twenty, and he was able to transition into being a full-time musician quickly. He was managing a surf shop on Clearwater Beach in 2013, and his boss retired. Chase received a little bit of severance pay, allowing him to spend about six months going to open mics and talking with other working musicians. One of them told him that he sounded great, and he just needed to get the equipment and learn about sixty songs. At the time, Chase recalls, he knew about twenty. So he started working on his repertoire and continued going to open mics. Every week he tried to learn and play five new songs. When he finally felt like he was ready, he was asked to play a gig.

It was at one of the places where he had been performing at their weekly open mic for about two months. The owner approached him and said that they had every other Wednesday open. Chase took the gig. A three-hour performance earned him money, free food and drinks. He recalled that he didn't have enough equipment yet, but he just took the gig and prayed for the best. It would work out. He told me he wouldn't recommend doing it that way now. But he was young, and his gear worked, and it was fun.

I asked him what kind of equipment he was using now, and he responded by saying that he was using better equipment than when he started. Right now, he is using a couple of QSC K12 speakers. He is thinking about adding a subwoofer for some of the bigger venues that he plays. He uses powered speakers, and has tried different mixers. Right now, he is using a PreSonus StudioLive AR8c, which is an eight-channel mixer.

Chase uses a Shure Beta 57 microphone, and a Martin DC16 dreadnought guitar. He doesn't think they make that model anymore, and I agree. I use a slightly older model Martin guitar, and they are not making mine anymore either. Chase said he has always loved Martin guitars for their deep tones and playability.

He's using a Boss 300 loop pedal. Next to it is a POG Octave pedal made by Electro-Harmonix. This helps him create bass guitar sounds for the bottom end of his loops. He also has a

Wah pedal, which I think is unique among acoustic players. He can combine the POG and the Wah to create funky Jerry Garcia-type tones for his guitar. Opening the Wah up to the thin treble tone and then adding the octave pedal can create cool sounds. He also has a Roland Handsonic percussion drum pad off to the side, and it also runs through the loop.

Pro Tip: *You can use clear tape to hold your foot pedal settings in place. The little knobs on your foot pedals can get turned during transit, and once you get them set where you want them, a little bit of clear masking tape over the top across all the dials of one pedal will hold the settings in place.*

I did ask him if he still plays songs with just voice and guitar, without all the effects and loops. He answered, "For sure, and it's probably like half-and-half throughout a gig." He added that he likes to start a gig without the loop involved, then mix it up. It's a way to add something to his show. We both have the same thought about mixing up the use of the looper by just having a rhythm guitar track to play over sometimes. We don't always add the bass lines and percussion sounds to every loop we make.

When I asked Chase how he picks songs to play, he explained that it seems to be whatever catches his ear throughout his day. He added that he tries to learn at least one new song every week, to keep it fresh for himself. Sometimes when he goes a whole month without learning a new song, he says that he starts to feel stale.

If something catches his ear on the radio, Pandora, Spotify, or someone asks for a good request that he doesn't know, he will try to learn the song. He will use the Shazam app, which identifies songs for the listener, if he hears something that he likes. Chase goes through his Shazam list on his phone at the end of each week to pick out songs to learn.

We talked about how as Solo Acoustic Musicians, we can get away with a lot in our interpretation of songs. What I mean by this is that we don't have to copy a song note for note from a recording. We can change the key or adapt the rhythm pattern to fit our unique singing and guitar playing style. Sometimes as a SAM, I can play with a chord chart and leave the individual note riffs out of a song. People should not expect a SAM to sound exactly like a recording, especially one full of other instruments like bass, drums, keys, horns, etc. Chase agreed and said, "You've got to make it your own. I think that's part of it. It's putting your style and taste into whatever song you feel like covering."

Chase said that he usually starts with the guitar part when writing original songs. Then the lyrics begin with a feeling. Once the guitar melody makes him feel a certain way, he will sit there and kind of freestyle words and/or sounds, trying to establish a melody and groove. Usually, one line will stick out a little bit, and often that is the hook that he will build the rest of the song around.

I finally remembered to ask him about his skateboard. I told him that I remembered the first time I saw him loading into a gig with speakers on his skateboard, and I asked him if he still did it that way. He said that he does, and we both laughed. He explained that people overlook the skateboard when it has speakers and other gear stacked on it. It just looks like any other type of dolly. When he is done unloading the equipment and gets on his skateboard to ride back to his car and get his guitar, people notice. He is still having fun with it. He admitted that he might get a cart someday, because he keeps adding more gear to his setup and making more trips to his vehicle.

We talked about the different distances to load in on gigs. Chase recently played a wedding at a large hotel on the beach in St. Petersburg. He arrived an hour early to load in, but wished he had come even earlier when he saw how much walking was involved, and the number of stairs he encountered. He said it was a nightmare; he felt rushed to get set up on time. It was just a cocktail hour, but it required an excessive amount of running around just for the load-in. He didn't say it, but I understood from my own experience that there was a little more riding on the gig than a typical night at a local dive bar. A wedding is a special event and a special day in someone's life.

Chase started playing on the west coast of Florida, in the Tampa Bay area where he grew up. Now he lives in Satellite Beach, between Melbourne and Cocoa Beach on the east coast. Cocoa Beach is famous for its space shuttle launches and cruise ship port. He moved about four years ago, when he was twenty-four years old.

He said, "Honestly, dude, it was a struggle at first. I moved over there for a few months. I was tired of playing the gigs here, and I felt I wanted to surf. I knew the cost of living over there was a little cheaper, and I was going over there to surf anyway. I would check around different bars over there. There was music going around, and beach bars were my style. I enjoy playing that reggae kind of stuff. I felt like it would be a good fit for me. I just needed a change at that time."

Chase told me that he moved there with a good demo that he had professionally recorded. The money he spent on that was an investment in himself. He shopped his demo around the east coast for about three months before moving, hitting up every place that he could find. His search included probably thirty-five to forty different venues. He would send them a good video, which was the demo he invested his money into making. It had five sections of songs on it, each one twenty-five seconds long. It wasn't a very long clip, just around two minutes.

He said that nobody got back to him right away, out of forty places. He had emailed everybody, called them and the venues, and got the emails of all the bookers. Finally, a few venues got back to him and told him they were booked full already. He countered by asking about further out in the calendar, for the next year, and was told they were fully booked. One place did get back to him with good news; four years later, he still plays there all the time. They have been good to him. He said, "They took a chance on me, which was fun, and yeah, it worked out."

Other than that, though, he had to rely on the same approach that helped him get gigs initially. So he started going to open mics in the area, met other local musicians and built a personal network. It happened quickly, according to Chase. He showed up on a Monday when a venue was having a singer-songwriter night and met other musicians. One of those guys had an open mic down the street the next day. So the next night, Chase went over there and played. It was good for him to go to these open mics, because that venue was looking for someone to play every Thursday night and offered him the spot, starting right away. Four years later, he still has that gig.

Eventually, he got more gigs through his network. He was randomly offered some chances to cover for other people. He feels that things became easier for him once his name got around town. He thinks it was about six months after moving that things started to get better for him. He said it took a toll on him for sure. He even considered moving back to the west coast, and was still playing gigs around here during his transition. The gigs weren't coming in quickly enough; he was making enough to pay the bills, but not making real money yet. He knew he wanted to stick it out, though, which he has done. He liked that area, and his dream was to play music while living on the beach. It was a rough start, but he hung in there and has carved out a spot for himself in Satellite Beach.

Recently, Chase went to St. Augustine, for a little bit of a staycation. It's just under a two-hour drive from his house going north up the coast. About a month before he went, he reached out to a musician friend who lived and played there. He asked him about the chance of getting a gig while he was in town. His friend lined him up with a Saturday fill-in spot at a venue. He told me that he enjoyed the gig and had fun. It was a new scene and a new crowd.

To promote his upcoming gigs, Chase will post a picture once a week that has dates, times, and locations listed. He shares this through his linked Instagram and Facebook pages, so he only has to do it once. He used to post one gig at a time in written text but now thinks that a picture in the background with his information layered on top is more eye-catching. I see his weekly posts, and I think they look great. I believe that he is right about how he is promoting his gigs.

Chase's tip can is a box that his brother-in-law made for him. He has put stickers on it, and it says "TIPS," and he has added his Venmo address. He says using apps like Venmo has become a common thing that SAMs should do now. It used to be a choice or preference, but we were all playing on live streams during the shutdowns, and this was how people could tip us. This has carried over into our in-person gigs. Also, an increasing number of people do not carry cash, and this is an easy way to make sure we still get a tip. I told him that people will walk by my table on their way out of a venue and take a picture of my tip can sign. Then they will Venmo me a tip later. Chase has also noticed this happening to him.

When someone from the audience walks up to ask Chase what kind of music he plays, he responds, "Good music." We both laugh. Every SAM I know does things differently, and Chase handles requests by doing his best to appease them if he can. Sometimes this means playing a song he doesn't particularly like, or stepping out of his comfort zone. He is a soft-spoken guy and will deal with aggressive requesters or hecklers with grace and dignity. I admire this about him.

In the beginning, Chase was focused on being a good musician, and now that he feels he has matured in that area, he tells me that he is finding ways of opening up to engage the audience and is trying to have more fun with his performance. He will try to talk to whoever looks like they enjoy what he is doing the most. Sometimes, he will start a dialogue with the closest table. He might ask them something like, "Where are you all from?" It's a simple icebreaker, and it works. He says part of what the venue pays for is for him to help people have an enjoyable time. If he misses a few notes, oh well. If people are smiling and having fun, then he is doing a good job. He used to be more critical of his music, but now he does it with a smile on his face. Chase is a good musician, and that's not going to change. But now, he is relaxed and having more fun with all aspects of performing.

> **Pro Tip:** *If you make a mistake during your performance, it's okay. Don't freak out, and don't stop the song! Just move on and finish. Finish the set. Finish the show. Make a mental note of your mistakes and try to perform better at the next one.*

There are many ways to have fun and engage your audience as a SAM. Sometimes changing the lyrics of a song can be fun. An example would be the song "Sitting On the Dock of the Bay" by Otis Redding. Instead of saying "Frisco bay," Chase replaces that with "Tampa Bay." He told me that a table of people ordered a round of tequila shots at a recent gig. So Chase played the riff to the song "Tequila." They loved it, and bought him a shot as well. People were smiling, laughing, and having a fun time. We both laughed when I said that "Tequila" is the best karaoke song ever.

Chase told me that he has been lucky when things go wrong on gigs. He has never had to pack up and leave a venue, which is good. Early on, his few mishaps were silly and embarrassing. He once forgot his mic stand and had to duct tape his microphone to the back of a chair, for example. Another time, he broke a string and didn't have a replacement, so he had to play an hour and a half while missing a string. I have done this before, and it's not fun to have to play this way. Another example would be having a cable stop working on a gig. None of these situations were major fiascos, but they were lessons in being prepared. He tries to bring a backup of everything he can. He always has extra cables. He always has two microphones with him. As far as his mic stands or speaker stands, he says they never leave his car.

Pro Tip: *Always have extra single strings or another pack of strings with you in case you break a string during your gig.*

Chase doesn't take risks with his equipment. He has lost a couple of mixers due to rain in the past. A friend had a two-thousand-dollar keyboard ruined by a sudden down-pour, and Chase learned from her experience. He tells me he had dealt with a few managers who got upset with him because he didn't want to play or wasn't willing to set up when the rain was coming. He even says that it turned into an argument at least once, but he stood his ground. He was fired from the place and taken off their calendar. Chase said to me that it's just not worth it. Of course, if you have read SAM1, you know I agree with Chase 100% and do not like to risk my equipment being damaged. As a SAM, you must stand up for yourself and protect your gear. I'm proud of Chase for being strong enough to do that. You can replace a gig or venue with a new one. It is harder to replace all your equipment.

On the east coast, Chase has been booking gigs by himself without the help of any agents. He finds that most venues oversee their booking with an in-house employee or man-ager. He expresses that he doesn't really like agents and has an issue with them taking money from the musicians. A cou-ple of agents he worked with before were paid by venues, and didn't charge the musicians. This kind of arrangement is okay, in his opinion.

Being nice to the employees at a venue goes a long way to get a SAM booked again. Quite often, patrons will say to the waitstaff that they liked the performer or, in some cases, that they didn't like the musical act. If you are friendly to the waitstaff and bartenders, they might give you a favorable review when a manager asks them what they think. Even if an audience member didn't like you, the server might ignore that information if *they* like you. This response can lead to more future bookings. The connection to a manager or owner happens in many ways, and these communications occur when we may not even know they are going on. Be on your best behavior, be humble, and do your best. A connection with your co-workers can help you.

Tipping the staff that takes care of you throughout a gig can be part of nurturing a relationship. If you always tip a bartender when you play at a venue, they will appreciate it and remember you for a good reason. On the other hand, if you are needy and order a lot of food and beverages and then don't leave a tip for them, it can be bad for you. Their opinion can sometimes make or break your deal. Just trying to be pleasant and professional can go a long way toward building your future. When I hear Chase talk about these things, I feel that he has matured into a seasoned veteran over his time as a SAM.

We discussed some gigs where we didn't have much fun. We talked about double bookings. We talked about arriving on time and waiting for people to finish eating so that an employee can move a table to create a place to set up. I will not run on about these things because they can carry a negative tone. I did enjoy hearing familiar experiences from another SAM, a friend and a peer on the music scene. It might be some venting and complaining, but they are shared experiences. It can be good to hear these things from other people living the same lifestyle.

Along with the negative part of the story, there can be a solution or resolution that we can share with our counterparts. It can be therapeutic to have these conversations, especially with someone who understands what you are talking about and what you have gone through. Chase confided in me that, in a way, it is a lonely job. You show up by yourself, you leave by yourself, and you don't have that camaraderie that most jobs or even bands have. He says, "You are kind of this lone wolf that travels around playing music."

What a musician charges or gets paid for a performance is a topic that is hard to talk about with other musicians. Finances are private, and it's hard to find friends who are comfortable disclosing that information. Chase and I were candid as we discussed conversations we have both had with owners or managers about their pay scale. Part of the Solo Acoustic Musician's job is sales and booking gigs for money. This will include negotiations with the people booking the talent for a venue. Understanding what you are worth and what venues are willing to pay is critical.

Chase has reached a point where he knows what he can do and what he should charge for his services. Although we didn't get into what any specific places pay, we did talk about fees we charge. Many factors can be involved, but some things are not always a part of the equation because each situation is different. How many hours of playing music, the day of the week, and the distance to the venue can affect your fee calculation. Demonstrating a high value during your performance is essential to validate the price that you charge. Negotiating with venues is a challenging part of our jobs. It's a never-ending process of learning more about sales to be better at getting booked as a Solo Acoustic Musician.

In my mind, Chase has had two beginnings of being a Solo Acoustic Musician. One happened here at his home by the beach in Tampa Bay, and the other occurred four years ago when he moved to the east coast of Florida, where he lives now. One thing Chase remembered along the way were the phone calls he received to go fill in for someone else and cover a gig. Many of those gigs became new venues that he could book himself into. Chase has done the right thing by reciprocating the gesture for those musicians who helped him and other musicians who needed a helping hand. He has helped other musicians get into venues he was already playing by telling the manager that they were good, or by getting them to cover a shift for him. That is one of his good character traits, and as a member of the lifestyle we share, he is giving back to his SAM community.

After 4 PM, we decided to part ways for the day. We have stayed in touch since. We don't get to hang out much because we are both gigging SAMs, so it was a lot of fun to sit down and talk about what we do for a living. Since he has been living on the east coast, it is even rarer for me to see him around town. So I thought it was great to spend a couple of hours with him and listen to his stories and see how he has grown into a successful Solo Acoustic Musician. I remember him starting his SAM journey, and I may have said a few things that helped guide him along the way, but he has done it all independently. He has taken advice from other musicians as well along the way and applied all the good things to carving out his musical world. He plays five shows a week steadily all year long and has fun living by the beach. Not too bad a way to live, if you ask me. I think he will continue to carry the torch of being a successful Solo Acoustic Musician for many years to come.

I am happy to call him my friend and I look forward to seeing what he does with his future.

You can find him on social media sites, and if you look on the beach, you can probably find him surfing.

VI. SCOTT "TWITCH" ANDERSON

Tuesday, August 10th, 2021, 6 PM
Middle Grounds, Treasure Island, FL

I know you are already wondering about the nickname "Twitch," and I will get to it, but I am trying to build suspense, so you will have to wait for an explanation.

I was stuck in traffic only a mile away from Middle Grounds because the John's Pass drawbridge was open, finally arriving right before 6 PM for dinner with an old friend. I have known Scott for almost as long as I have lived here in Florida. We met at a singer-songwriter open mic with an emphasis on original music, hosted at a listening room in St. Petersburg. I used to go there every Tuesday night to play my original songs and listen to the other musicians. I bought one of Twitch's CDs, and had it in my car for years. He was an outstanding performer, and I looked forward to hearing him perform his songs at the open mic.

The hostess showed us to a booth off to the dining room side, away from the lounge, and we settled in for dinner and a conversation. I started by asking Scott when he started playing guitar and how he became a Solo Acoustic Musician. He told me that he learned guitar later than he thinks most people who do this for a living started. Most of the SAMs he knows started playing guitar when they were eight to ten years old, played with other musicians in high school, and were in bands. They would spend time learning and playing songs by other people, but never write songs of their own. Scott explained that he did not start to play guitar until he was about twenty, and as soon as he began learning, he also started writing songs. His career started right there.

Scott is sixty-one years old and has decades of experience playing the guitar. He confided to me that he never learned a cover song until he was forty years old. He added that he had a profound experience with Christianity, and that his writing reflected his experience at that time in his life. Almost all of it was related to his faith, personal life, health, and how God interacted with the whole thing. At the same time, he was pretty removed from what would be considered the traditional church, because he grew up in an extremely strict environment like that. He always felt that it was probably more of a hindrance than a help to many people because of particular leaders in charge of those churches. His songwriting was in line with his faith and personal life experiences pouring out of him and into his music.

Eventually, this led him into the Christian music world, where his career took off. He was still new to writing when he attended a songwriting event in Colorado. Industry people gathered there, and musicians could pitch songs. Scott won a first place and a second place songwriting award. A small independent label heard his music, and he signed a deal with them. At this point, he had already recorded the songs for the record on his own. He added three more tracks for a total of eleven songs. This small label released the record and distributed it worldwide. That launched him to where music became what he could do full time. He recalls that it was 1988, and he was twenty-eight years old when he finished the record. In 1989 he started going full-time with his music career. He went on tour with a Christian rock band, serving as the opening act for all their shows.

Scott became interested in sharing his music with the youth market, so he went to the National Youth Workers Convention. People from around the world come to this event once a year. He secured an exhibit space to give away promotional materials to youth leaders, youth pastors, and others. He would book out his calendar from his networking at this conference every year. Let me repeat that: Scott booked his whole year's worth of gigs from attending this one event.

Scott was doing his own booking and managing himself. This was before cell phones, email, and the internet. He used to have to send out physical contracts and get physical checks back in the mail for his deposits. He would prepare a trip, take it, and then come home. He would finalize his details for the next trip, the one after that, on to the third, fourth, and even fifth one after that. Scott was always preparing several trips out. I can see how this would be like a cycle of getting things in order and then executing each trip as a plan of action—continuing to plan more trips based on the calendar's bookings. It sounded to me like a lot of information and responsibilities for one person to juggle.

He admitted that it was exhausting, because he was not only arranging everything, but he had to sell. He built a database of leads from people who came to his booth and showed an interest in booking him. But he still had to be selling and following up with those contacts. He was dealing with a variety of clients with different budgets. Some people would love to have him play at their church, but they were too small. He would try to figure out ways to accommodate the smaller events or churches into a more significant trip. What he would do was look at one gig as his anchor date. If he had a gig that paid well and would cover the trip's expenses, he could add shows to his calendar around that date. He could travel out, playing gigs before and after the anchor show. This method of booking also allowed him to work with smaller venues and varying budgets.

Pro Tip: *Always warm up your voice before the gig. I'm in my car on the way to a gig, doing warm-up exercises—every gig. I never skip it.* — Scott "Twitch" Anderson

---

While he was doing all of this, his first record was released, and thirteen thousand units were shipped out to retail stores. His CD was distributed to and sold in Christian bookstores, which were the retail outlet for all things religious, including music, in the Christian market. My mom was a church organist, so I shared with Scott that I knew the kind of store he was talking about and had been to plenty of them when I was growing up. Eventually, Scott made a second record, where he was once again responsible for all the production costs. The label that had signed him up for the first record went out of business; they were a tiny company and didn't manage their finances very well. Scott's album was finished, but he had nowhere to go with it.

A former employee of the first label moved to another, more prominent company based in Newport Beach, California, and became the president of their distribution side. That label also oversaw distribution for about ten other, smaller Christian music labels. So the guy Scott knew got him a meeting with an A&R guy at the new label. Scott said that the A&R guy was as pompous as could be when they talked. They did want to sign him, though, and presented him with an offer. The terms were terrible, and he told them that he would never sign a deal like the one they offered him that day. It didn't faze the pompous A&R guy, who told Scott "if you don't, there are a hundred other people who will sign up for a deal like this." Scott held firm to his decision and chose not to accept the offer. What he ended up doing was calling the guy he knew on the distribution side of this company. He pitched the idea that his record is finished and asked, why didn't they do a distribution deal? He would function as his own label. The company wouldn't have to spend any money out of pocket for production and just collect money on the distribution side. They worked on the terms, and finally the label was willing to do a distribution deal.

At that point, Scott was doing everything: booking, management, retail sales, and all the other things that a record label would do for him. He told me that one of the crazy ideas he discovered in the business is that these labels would spend advertising dollars based on a projected number of sales. They based this number on historical data for the sales of new artists' releases. He explained further that this meant they took a number that they averaged out and decided based on that information. Scott did not agree with this idea at all. Since he was in control of his advertising budget, he decided to "blow the socks off this thing and put his face out there like you wouldn't believe." He told me he spent a good chunk of money doing just that.

The Gospel Music Association has an annual event in Nashville, and Twitch went there to support his new CD. Other veteran artists and people who were top names in the industry knew who he was because of his advertising efforts. Some of them approached him to say that his face was everywhere, and they wanted to know to which label he was signed. His answer was that he was his own label. He told me that they were confused by his response, and he had to explain to them that he had a distribution deal through a company. So all the advertisements they were seeing were being paid for by him. These people knowing who he was and approaching him was validation for his financial commitment and his risk in doing things differently. Scott told me that it totally paid off.

He told me how much money labels would spend on advertising based on the projected sales numbers for a new artist's first release. He says if they expected to sell 5500 units, they knew how much money they would make and budgeted a percentage of that number for advertising. Scott says that he more than doubled the amount of money that the label would have spent on advertising. His original shipment was 17,000 units. The guy at the distribution company that brought Scott on board believed in him and knew how hard he worked. He told Scott that he was the talk of the company, and that he had sold three times as much as any of their new artists. Scott said that it was because he advertised more. What was so hard about understanding that?

Unfortunately, the man running the whole company made bad choices and managed money very poorly. He eventually ran the company into the ground. One day when people showed up to work, there was a padlock on the door. The company was so far into debt that it couldn't continue. Scott no longer had distribution for his record. It was only a few months after the release and wasn't even in the second quarter of sales yet. He did what he could do to fulfill the rest of the orders placed by stores. However, he couldn't take his record to another company for distribution because the most significant money to be made was in the front end with those

17,000 units. Scott explained that he might trickle out with another 10,000 units in the next year. Another company would want to make money off the first orders of a new release. That's where the biggest money will always be made in a distribution deal. Scott had already shipped out 17,000 units and would now get smaller orders over time. Also, because his label was just him, he didn't have a roster of other artists to bring to a potential distributor. If he had another six or ten other artists signed that he could include in a deal, it might have been worth it to another company.

Another major thing that Scott did that was brilliant was keeping ownership of his masters. If he had taken the first deal, the one he rejected, he would have probably lost ownership of his recordings. Retaining ownership of his masters, he could make duplicates at dirt cheap prices. He was paying about 65 cents a CD. Including packaging, his unit cost was about $1.20, and he could sell his CDs for about $13 retail. He says that that money kept him going. Even after the distribution company fell apart, Scott continued playing live and promoting his music. He still went to the youth workers convention every year and could book gigs as he did before. The distribution deal didn't last long, but it had given him greater prominence in the industry, which helped him fill his calendar.

His first record was released in 1989, and the second in 1992, and Scott continued supporting his original music through 2004. He called it being a road dog. His anchor dates were generally large churches, where he would come in and do a youth concert. They might also let him take part in their morning or evening Sunday services. He told me that these were mega-churches. I can only imagine what it was like, based on what I have seen on TV. I grew up in a small church atmosphere.

The churches knew that he made most of his money from CD sales and would let him put his music for sale out in the lobby. He would sell a single CD for $13 or $25 for both. Sometimes he would sell hundreds of CDs at one gig. The church was also compensating him for his travel over and above the performance fee. He could make thousands of dollars playing his original music for large audiences in the churches in one weekend. Some months he would play a lot of gigs, which would be very lucrative. Typical of sales or gig work, though, he also had valleys where things were slow for months.

Scott was approaching forty and was getting a little burnt out from traveling around the country for gigs. He realized he hadn't gotten the breaks he needed to make it to another level. Twitch lived in California's San Francisco Bay area for years and then moved to L.A. at the end of 1995. He wanted to expand beyond the Christian marketplace. He was trying to get his music accepted as art, and not just because of its message. In the Christian music world, the message is kind of hand in hand with the music, and he wanted to be able to get some songs out there where he didn't write about faith or God. He told me that when he moved to L.A., he had close calls but never got the door open.

As he was about to turn forty, things changed for him with the youth market in which he had been so successful. The people in charge of hiring were getting younger, and the music was changing drastically. Scott realized that he was aging out of the Christian youth music market. He had to figure out something.

At one point in the early eighties, Twitch had lived in the Tampa area for two years. Also, every year he would come to Florida for ten days to two weeks for gigs and would stay at a friend's house in St. Petersburg. He would play at youth church events in Fort Lauderdale, Naples, and Fort Myers. He would also go to Lake City, Jacksonville, and Orlando on trips. He told me how he used to love to get a newspaper at lunchtime and sit down and read the local news when he was traveling. When he started looking at the property prices, he couldn't believe what he saw. The friend he was staying with happened to be a real estate broker. So he discussed the low real estate prices with him. There was a considerable difference between the California prices that he was used to seeing and what was available in Florida. His friend also knew another friend who was high up in a mortgage bank and could help Scott with financing. After a couple of visits to look at properties, he bought a house and moved to Florida in 1999.

A significant factor in his decision to move here was knowing he could make a living playing music here. He had seen many Solo Acoustic Musicians working here and knew that he could get gigs if he learned cover songs. When he arrived in Florida, he was still making his trips for church gigs, and would continue to do them as he transitioned into a new life. During the first couple of years of living here, that was what he did. He would leave town for several days at a time for gigs.

Pro Tip: *Always have a towel. It's a hard job, and it's hot inside and outside. As a SAM, you will sweat, so always have a towel and a backup towel. Always buy two.*

Scott was hanging out at a popular bar and met some other musicians. One of them invited him to come to another bar with him, and that was where he met a musician who has been on the local circuit for decades. When someone would ask Twitch, "Where do you play?", he would explain about his travel gigs and events. He could tell people weren't sure if he was telling the truth or not.

The musician asked him if he wanted to get up and play a couple songs that night. He replied that he didn't know any cover songs. The other man invited him up anyway. So Twitch played a couple of his songs. Now that these two guys had heard him play, they would routinely invite Twitch to play a couple of songs whenever he was around. On one of these nights, an owner of another popular bar nearby was there.

The owner was impressed and invited him to come to play music at his bar down the street. Twitch explained that he would love to but didn't know cover songs. The owner was impressed by the music and the customers' reaction, and wanted to hire Twitch regardless. He offered him a week-end gig for all the nights. So he filled in his calendar for the weekends when he wasn't traveling, all because of this new contact he made while networking with other musicians and sharing his music. This booking worked for a little while, but his road gigs took him away. One stretch had him in Ocean City, MD, for a weekend and then three weeks in Australia, followed by a weekend in Portland, OR. Five weekends in a row that he would be out of town. He communicated this to the bar owner and gave him plenty of notice so he could cover those shows.

Now that he had the bar gig, he started to learn cover songs. He began focusing on songs he already knew the words to because he'd heard them so often over the years. He also stuck to learning songs that he liked. He admitted to me that he doesn't always learn songs note for note, like the original recording. I smiled at this, because I am the same way, in that I will take a cover and kind of make it my own. I think this approach is fun; it's about being comfortable as a performer and providing a unique version of a song.

Twitch continued to see his new musician friends on his nights off, and he would often be asked to perform a few songs. On another one of these nights, he was approached by a bartender in charge of booking the music at one of the hotel resorts in St. Pete Beach. Once again, Twitch told this new contact that he didn't know a lot of cover songs, and once again, he was greeted with the words, "That's great!" The bartender told Twitch that they heard the same cover songs seven nights a week and that it would be nice to hear something new. This chance meeting turned into a steady gig that lasted sixteen years.

He continued to learn cover songs as he went, adding songs here and there and keeping his repertoire fresh. As he settled into life in Florida, he could wean himself off touring and become a full-time local SAM. He told me that every one of his gigs allowed him to play his original songs and that he never received any negative response from venues. Having his CD by his tip jar and singing his original songs still worked for him to sell units on the local gigs. He would jokingly announce to the audience that he would play a few original songs, and if they put ten dollars in his tip jar, the CD was free. "Marketing Genius!", he would exclaim. The bartenders loved it, and of course, the audience became engaged with him and his music. This saying became a signature for him when working the crowd and selling his merchandise.

Twitch became extremely busy on the local scene and explained that, especially during the season, he could be doing doubles five days a week and singles on the other two days for months at a stretch. That is twelve gigs a week and no days off. That is a busy musician! He eventually scaled it back to seven gigs a week, with at least one day off, by only doing double shifts on the weekend. At this point, he began to take the money he had been making and invest in property to develop rental income. He has tried to convey this to the younger musicians he meets when they are coming up. He says, "The money will be good sometimes. The money will be bad sometimes. What you do with it will make a difference to you. You have to learn to budget, and you have to learn to invest it in something that will generate income for you." Twitch is currently playing four gigs a week while also collecting rent on his properties. He doesn't have to play twelve gigs a week anymore. I think it was a smart move.

Scott is currently using thirty-year-old EV twelve-inch speakers made from old wood-style cabinets. He said that it makes a difference for him and that the tone is much warmer than the newer plastic speaker boxes. He has had them re-coned and repaired over the years to keep them usable while also sounding good. He has used a Mackie 808S powered mixer to run the P.A. for about twenty years. This unit has built-in effects, and Scott only uses reverb. The main guitar that he uses for his gigs is a 1991 Takamine FP-360SC cutaway, and this is his third one.

On arrival for one gig at a beach hotel resort, Scott had just pulled up to unload when he was greeted by one of the bartenders. This bartender loved Scott's music and was excited that he was playing that night. He was so excited, he offered to help unload Scott's gear. The bartender grabbed Scott's guitar, which was in a soft case, and leaned it on the side of the car. Scott hadn't gotten out of the vehicle yet, and didn't notice what the bartender did with his guitar. He told the guy to please not help him unload anything because he has a system for unloading his gear.

Scott told me that everything goes on his cart a certain way and that he will put his cart off to the side, park his car and walk back with his guitar. It was nighttime, and his car interior was black. The soft case for his guitar was black, too. So he unloaded his car, filled up his cart, and pushed it down the driver's side of the car toward the sidewalk. He got back in the car to back up and go park. He tells me that he turned the wheel and then heard a sort of whooshing, sliding sound. He thought, "What was that?", but he kept backing up and heard a louder noise like wood crunching. The bartender was standing in front of his car with his eyes wide open and a weird look on his face. Scott turned to look at his back seat, and his guitar was not there. So, this first sound was probably his guitar sliding down the side of the car, and the second sound was Scott backing over the guitar in its soft case. Needless to say, Scott doesn't like people to help him load or unload. He has a system in place and is very protective of his gear.

He found another guitar online that was the same model, but a 1994 edition. He played this guitar on many gigs, and it has the wear to prove it. Last winter, he bought another 1991 edition on eBay. It was in mint condition. He told me that he is never using a soft case again. He put the new 1991 guitar in a hard case, and the 1994 model has become his backup guitar.

As with the other musicians I've interviewed, rain is a major concern for Scott. He told me about a three-day-a-week residency he has been playing for about five years. He feels extremely fortunate to have this gig because the manager really likes him and his music. She is also very understanding about the weather situation. She gets it. She still pays him if his shift is canceled due to weather. He says that she understands that if he has reserved this time for them, he can't go do something else because it's raining. His opinion is that every venue should have this policy for the musicians. I have to say, this is a Holy Grail type of gig situation. In a way, it's like he is on salary at this place. It is almost unheard of to be paid for a gig rain or shine.

Scott said that he constantly has his phone on the radar for the weather when he is on an outdoor gig. A rain cell can develop overhead out of nowhere, and rain can start falling before it even shows up on the radar satellite reading on his phone. He has been rained on before, and there are also times when he can see dark clouds in the distance, and he will look at his phone to see if it's visible on radar and which way it is moving. Every outdoor gig where there is a possibility of rain, his phone is right next to him with the weather radar turned on. Sometimes he will take a minute to look at it in between songs because he is trying to figure out what the weather is doing and how it might affect his gig. Because of this issue, he tries to book a balanced percentage of indoor and outdoor gigs.

You probably think I've forgotten to tell you about Scott's nickname. When he did youth events earlier in his career, he talked about overcoming personal obstacles and how his faith played a part in that. He would tell the crowd how his biggest obstacle was living with Tourette's syndrome. People would respond by telling him that he had given them hope for their child, who might be dealing with some form of adversity. Some of them were even dealing with one of their children having Tourette's. Scott realized that he should bring this more into the forefront of what he was doing. He decided to give himself the nickname "Twitch" and named his record *Twitch*. He contacted the National Tourette Syndrome Association in Queens, NY, sending them a CD with a letter explaining who he was. They invited him to play at their international conference. After that, he began doing more events with them. The association has a summer camp, and Twitch would go and sing for them. He tells me that there are different degrees of Tourette's syndrome, and each person is unique. I think it's a cool nickname.

Every interview I had done before this was during the afternoon, but this one was at dinnertime and ended with dessert before we parted ways. There was a pretty good SAM in the lounge, providing background music for our dinner meeting. I had a really enjoyable time learning new things about Scott and finding out about his early days, which were quite different from most of us local SAMs. I have a feeling that he will continue playing his guitar and singing songs for people here on the beach for a long time.

Visit his website to listen to or purchase his music online: Twitch.us

VII. CHARLES SCROGGINS (LUTHIER)

Monday, August 9th, 2021, 2PM
Bahama Breeze, Lutz, FL

Life throws us curveballs sometimes. Charles and I arrived at our original choice of meeting place, and they were closed. So we headed for another spot nearby, only to find that they were closed, too. Our third choice was a home run, and we were happy to finally find our way to an air-conditioned spot to sit and talk. It was scorching out that day, as it can be in August in Florida. We grabbed a booth inside and started talking.

Charles told me right off the bat that his specialty is building and maintaining acoustic and electric instruments. He does neck-throughs, set necks, bolt-ons — any guitar style. He also works on and builds archtops. Charles explained that the archtop is modeled after the violin, with a hollow body, and instead of one sound hole, like a regular acoustic guitar, it has two F-holes. He told me some specifics about how the neck extends across the body like a violin, and there is a difference from other guitars in the bracings. He can work on mandolins and banjos, but he doesn't build those instruments.

I asked Charles how and when he became a luthier. He went back to the beginning and said that he liked to take his toys apart and put them back together as a kid. Why does this work that way? How does this work? Oh, this toy is doing something extraordinary, but how does it move that way? These are questions he would ask himself, and then try to find the answers. He would pull something apart to watch the gears, etc. He said that's just how his brain works. These were the types of things that he found satisfying.

When he was around eleven, he picked up a guitar and started to play music. Of course, one of the things that he wanted to do was figure out how it worked. It was in his early twenties that he became a luthier. Charles is forty-six now, and has been building, fixing, and maintaining guitars as a luthier professionally for over twenty years.

Being a luthier also includes taking them apart and putting them back together. He has also been fabricating guitars from scratch, from his own original designs. Sometimes, he may also need to fabricate a part when repairing an instrument. I asked him more about this, and he gave me an example. Sometimes, he may have to remove a guitar's bridge during a neck reset. The bridge holds the saddle, the white piece that fits into the slot. During a neck reset, he may have to move the saddle, which means he most likely will also have to replace the bridge. This explanation sounds very technical, but we have to remember that a guitar requires precise measurements for its pieces to work together correctly. To take a new piece of wood and work with it to create a new bridge is indeed a top-notch skill. After he removes the original bridge, he can use it as a template to help him make the new one. It can be even more complicated than my description. Charles knows what he is talking about, for sure.

Charles moved from Texas to the West Palm Beach area when he was seventeen. He found his way to the north Tampa Bay area of Land O' Lakes when he was about twenty-three years old. In Texas, he had been in bands as a multi-instrumentalist, just as he is today. He plays guitar, bass, and most instruments with strings, and has even learned to play the drums. He is a luthier and builds, repairs, and maintains instruments for other people as a career, but he is also a musician who loves to play music.

He found himself working in different music stores as a luthier. After a while, he opened his very own guitar repair shop. He was in an upstairs unit of an office building for about ten years. He is currently the luthier at a music store in Clearwater, Florida. He told me that he is so busy that he could use another luthier or helper there. I asked him to estimate how many guitars he might work on in a day, a week, or a month. He said he will work on at least three guitars every day.

Charles pointed out that some jobs take more time than others, and sometimes it can be easy to get simple jobs done quickly. If someone drops off a guitar to be restrung and set up, that is easier than a fret dress or fret replacement, which takes a lot more time to complete. He estimated that around a hundred and fifty guitars a month come across his workbench, adding that it's always more than a hundred.

Charles said that he did the math one time, and he is sure that over a ten-year span, he worked on more than ten thousand guitars. I think that would probably put him in an expert category. During our conversation, he said something that revealed his humility and desire to learn more — that he is always looking to improve on what he is doing or discover something new from someone or another source. He also shared that he has learned from many people over the years. This is admirable, because it takes a lot to admit we don't know everything and seek out more knowledge. This self-examination helps us grow and become better at our chosen professions.

One thing Charles wanted to make sure I included is that he believes it is essential that every guitar player should know how to adjust the neck of their guitar. I will admit that

I am not proficient at this, and I think that I have some work to do. He told me that it can weather once your guitar has been adjusted and set up. I think I know what he means by this. A guitar kind of changes with its environment and may need adjustments. He says he can make neck adjustments seasonally, weekly, or monthly. He added that it shouldn't be a sixty-dollar trip to the luthier every time the weather changes. This thought makes me envy all those pro touring guitar players who have the advantage of a guitar tech who does this for them every day.

Pro Tip: *Learn to adjust the neck of your guitar. — Charles Scroggins*

For a basic neck adjustment, he tells me to adhere to the simple rule of thumb when turning the wrench: righty-tighty and lefty-loosey. Another critical part of this process is string tension. He went into some specific things to do with certain types of guitars. My advice would be to ask someone to show you how to do this, or access YouTube videos on the subject. I do not want to explain some of what he just said and have you try to understand what it means and end up damaging your guitar. It's not that difficult to learn, but my explanation would not be as accurate as a hands-on demonstration that you can watch. I agree that knowing this information and having this skill takes your abilities to the next level.

Some new guitars will come with a little tool to access the truss rod and adjust the neck. If you buy a guitar and it comes with one of these, you should study how to use it properly. I have a Taylor guitar that came with one, and Charles told me everything I could do with it. One end is a screwdriver that fits perfectly into the tiny screws that hold the wood panel in place, hiding the bolt that hides my truss rod from sight. It's at the headstock of my guitar by the nut. Don't forget, righty-tighty and lefty-loosey.

It takes years of building and repairing guitars to get to Charles' level of expertise. He explained how easily a guitar can be affected by the weather in the middle of a gig. For example, even when the frets have been leveled and dressed, and the instrument has been properly set up, you can go out to play your gig at the beach, and the neck will absorb all the humidity and go haywire and straighten out. So it would be helpful if you knew how to loosen your guitar's truss rod to get your strings to ring clearly.

I asked him if he thought the situation could be that drastic in the middle of a gig, and he said it was possible. I have probably just played through this scenario many times without realizing it. Sometimes on a gig, we must put up with certain things that are uncomfortable just to get through the show. But if you have the ability to adjust your neck on the fly, you can make an uncomfortable situation go away with relative ease. That would be taking your skills to another level. Improving your sound is part of the product you are selling at a gig.

It is essential to let your guitar adjust to the room temperature for indoor gigs. For an outside gig, it is vital to be able to deal with the atmospheric variables. Charles says that even something as small as a cloud passing overhead and dropping the temperature briefly could cause a change in the guitar, and knock it out of tune. I never thought of it like that, but it does make sense. He told me that the strings are hypersensitive to changes in temperature and humidity. So the tiny difference between being in direct sunlight and then being set down in the shade during a SAM's break can be enough to affect the guitar. Charles once again reiterated that he considers the ability to make a neck adjustment a necessity for a Solo Acoustic Musician.

I asked Charles about things that would be good for a SAM to invest in to make their guitar better. Most guitars come out of the factory with plastic nuts and saddles. The nut is the white part at the top of the neck, by the headstock and tuning pegs, sitting near your fretting hand. The saddle is the white part on the bridge by the sound hole and pick guard (if you have one), where your picking hand will be. I talked with him about upgrading from plastic to bone, and he explained a few things.

The nut affects the open strings and the harmonics. It also affects the tuning stability. Bone is a much harder material than the plastics typically used for these pieces. It is also more slippery, improving the guitar's tuning stability. The soft plastics can dampen the sound by absorbing more of the energy out of the strings. Bone is a better material for nuts and saddles because it does not absorb the strings' energy as much, which improves the tone. Also, because the bone is a harder material, it will last longer than plastic. An upgrade like this would currently cost about two hundred dollars for both nut and saddle, and would also include a setup. I would recommend buying a new set of strings to have put on during this process.

A less obvious upgrade would be to investigate what kind of input jack you have and see if it can be improved. It's not so obvious because it's hidden beneath what we see all the time. Each guitar manufacturer will probably use a particular brand and type of input jack. Guitars have various levels of price and quality based on the materials and accessories used when they're built. An acoustic-electric guitar has an input jack to plug your guitar cable into and run to your pedalboard or the P.A. mixer. There are varying degrees of price points and levels of quality for input jacks. Buying a more expensive and higher-quality input jack can create a better tone and over-all sound from your guitar. You can ask a luthier to help you identify what is currently in your guitar, and you can also ask them to help figure out the options available for an upgrade. You'll want to get guidance and help to make the right choice. I would also suggest hiring your local luthier to install your new input jack, so you can be confident that it is done correctly.

Another basic upgrade for an acoustic guitar would be to have better frets installed. Most frets will come from the fac-tory in a type of brass called nickel silver. This is brass with nickel added to it to make the color silver. There are different specific percentages of nickel that produce different grades of nickel silver frets. Twenty-one percent is the highest and most durable. These frets wear down over time, especially if you play a lot, and will eventually need to be replaced, which is one of the tasks that a luthier does. After years of playing my Martin guitar, I wore down my factory frets and needed a repair. When I went to Charles, I decided to ask about an upgrade, and this is what he told me.

If you don't mind a slight change to your tone and want your frets to last forever, you want to upgrade to stainless steel frets. Charles told me it costs about four hundred dol-lars. This upgrade includes removing the old frets and leveling out any bumps and dips in the fretboard. Because stainless steel is a much more rigid material, the factories don't want to use them on all the guitars — it wears down the tools much faster. Nickel silver is an excellent metal for guitar frets and is the industry standard. I chose to make the upgrade because I play a lot of gigs and make my living with my guitar, and I wanted to extend the life span of my frets by installing the more durable stainless-steel frets.

Some people are allergic to nickel, and they can replace their frets with gold-colored EVO fret wire that is hypoallergenic. I had never heard of these frets, but I am glad to share this information with you in case you ever meet someone who has an allergic reaction to playing their guitar. Maybe they could get tested for a nickel allergy and switch out their frets.

Charles told me that a luthier can make an acoustic guitar sound remarkably like an electric guitar by setting the string action exceptionally low to the fretboard. Doing this will make the strings extremely easy to press down. He used to do re-fret jobs for fingerstyle players who wanted extra-low action. Different players can be particular about what they like and enjoy. When someone brings their guitar to him for adjustments or repairs, he always asks them how they play. His goal is to make their guitar play the way they want it to play, so they don't have to worry about that when going onstage. He said that he wants to take the guitar out of the way of their performance, and explained that some people want to fight the strings — to pick through them as they strum — and that it doesn't feel good unless the action is higher. For the most part, though, people ask him to make them as low as possible.

Pro Tip: *Check your strings every week before leaving your house to start your gigs for the week. Do you need to put on new ones? For years, I would put on a new set of strings every Tuesday, and then I would play the next five nights straight. It felt great to have fresh strings on my guitar every week.*

As Solo Acoustic Musicians, we network with other musicians in our areas and online. I asked Charles if there is a luthier community. He told me that it has been both friendly and competitive, in his experience. There are other luthiers where we live. The Tampa Bay area includes four counties and is home to over three million people. We have a lot of guitar players and a need for luthiers, so we have several nearby. I know of at least ten, and I am sure there are some more here. He told me there were times when it seemed like they all hated each other, but that changed. Now everyone seems to like each other. There are so many guitars that need repairs that one guy can't do it all. It's better to have a sense of community and help each other. Charles is so busy that he hopes to hire another luthier to work beside him at the store.

I asked Charles about another luthier in our area who recently passed away. This man had fixed a crack in my Martin years ago and was a nice guy. His house was full of guitars, and some of the ones hanging on the wall were incredibly old. Charles had never met him, but he described a guitar that he built for a man. Another luthier had appraised that guitar for its owner for insurance protection. He filled out the appraisal report and told the owner that it was worth twenty-five thousand dollars. It was a Celtic-themed guitar with inlays and silverwork done with the tuning machines. It had an exceptional fret job with inlays through the fretboard. Charles told me that it had all kinds of fancy stuff. The bridge pins had emeralds in them. I wish I had a picture of this guitar for the book. It sounds incredible.

I asked him about basic home maintenance or care advice. The first thing he said was that the best place to store a guitar is in its case. It's the most stable environment for a guitar and the best protection against any accidents.

Accidental damage can be a big deal. The next bit of advice was to always keep your guitar out of direct sunlight. I thought at once of the pictures I see of people who've hung their guitars on the wall. What if they are in direct sunlight for hours during the morning or the evening? Remember this tip if you want to hang your guitar on the wall or put one on a stand in the living room for easy access. Try to find a good spot without direct sunlight.

Your acoustic guitar can get too humid, or it can dry out. Both have to do with the guitar's environment. Charles tells me that every guitar is different, but all react to environmental changes to various degrees. Some guitars are more sensitive than others when it comes to temperature or humidity. If you use a dehumidifier in a room or a studio and go too far, that can be bad. He told me of a person using a dehumidifier and getting the humidity down to ten percent. Then they brought in their instruments from another room. Some of the guitars cracked from the drastic change in humidity. This example is extreme and rare, but it can happen.

He repeated that every guitar is different. He described one as bulletproof and said he could do anything to it without it being affected. He says that he could put it in the trunk of his car, and when he took it out, it would still be in tune. Another guitar might go haywire, and the neck could move if you breathed on it. Ask yourself, how sensitive is your guitar on a scale from one to ten?

Charles brought up the subject of cables and had this to say. "Long cables have something called capacitance which dampens the tone and makes them sound muddy. The longer the cable, the more capacitance it has, and it can interact with tone and volume controls for acoustic and electric guitars." I told him that I heard Eric Johnson, a well-known guitar player, would only use eighteen feet or less of cable because it changed the tone. Eric is particular about his gear. Charles confirmed that, saying that a difference can be noticeable to a discerning ear after twenty feet of cable.

I did some research for you, and while there is more to find out about this subject, if you want to look things up and learn more after reading my notes, you can start with questions like these. See how far you can go to understand what capacitance is and how it affects your guitar tone.

Capacitance: the ability of a system to store an electric charge.

What is capacitance in a guitar cable?

Capacitance describes the ability of two conductors, separated by an insulating material, to store charge. It is measured in picofarads per meter (pF/m) or picofarads per foot (pF/ft). It is also cumulative. For example, a cable rated at 100 pF/m that is 5 meters long will have a total capacitance of 500 pF/m.

What should the capacitance reading of a guitar cable be?

A proper cable should measure a capacitance value of 100 pF per meter. A 20 cm patch cable should give you a reading of around 20 pF, and the reading can be quite a bit higher without it, if there's anything wrong with the cable.

Does cable length affect guitar tone?

With a high-impedance guitar output, the greater the distance between your guitar and your amp, the more your tone will be affected by the resistance in the cable that's connecting the two. The longer the cable, the more the tone is affected negatively.

What is the best guitar cable length?

It's just common sense: the longer a distance your signal has to travel, the weaker it will get. The best bet is to stick to a length somewhere around fifteen feet. (We have established an under-twenty-feet rule with Charles, and most cables are fifteen, eighteen, or twenty feet long. For live performances, any of these should offer more than enough length to move around onstage a little bit.)

What is a low capacitance guitar cable?

The ZEROCAP ultra-low capacitance cable lets you hear all the frequencies your guitar produces. Cable capacitance kills the high frequencies from your pickups, resulting in a muddy sound. The ZEROCAP cable makes your guitar think it is driving about one foot of cable, and the sound opens up amazingly. (I cannot endorse this product personally, because I have never used it, but according to the information I found in my search, it does sound like it would be good for dealing with capacitance.)

Do guitar cables affect sound quality?

The electrical resistance of a guitar cable is insignificantly tiny compared with the impedance of the pickups and controls, so that won't affect your tone a great deal, but cable capacitance is another matter altogether. (Basically, it's not going to matter which distance cable or brand you use unless you have a very sensitive ear for tone. I suggest trying different ones and seeing if you can tell the difference. Pick which one sounds best to you and use that on your gigs.)

There is more to all of this, of course, and the information is out there. I hope this information gets you started learning about the role of guitar cables in the world of a Solo Acoustic Musician.

Charles added that an active circuit would make the cable's capacitance not a factor. So, you could use as long a cable as you want. He added that he thinks Eric Johnson uses passive pickups, which is why he uses less than twenty feet of cable from his guitar to his amp. I am afraid you may have some more research ahead, depending on how in-depth you want to learn about electricity and your guitar.

I'll get you started with this tidbit: active circuits have a buffer that lowers the output impedance and isolates the system from such loading effects. You can use long cables or pass your signal through several pedals without losing much of the original signal.

An active tone control circuit uses a battery-powered pre-amplifier, which allows us to boost and cut frequency bands.

If I were you, I would research your guitar and see if you have active or passive circuitry. I would also recommend asking someone at your music store about this, especially if you are buying a new guitar from them. The battery pack is one rule of thumb to tell the difference between passive and active. Does the guitar have a battery in it? That means it's active.

I added all this technical talk about capacitance to reveal all the thought and technical precision of being a luthier. I didn't even go all the way down the well. There is specific information to research if you want to pursue this as a career.

I have one or two guitars to keep track of and maintain. A guy like Charles could be fixing more than one hundred guitars a month, so he must know all the minute details about guitars and how they are played. It's impressive that he knows all this information, and uses it to help people maintain their instruments and make a living playing music.

I asked Charles if people ever brought him something that was beyond repair. He says that sometimes people will bring him a guitar from the Sixties that is way past being fixed up; the fretboard can be crumbly, the electronics are dust, or maybe termites have gotten into the wood. He mentions that it is becoming increasingly common these days, as these guitars are just getting older and older.

People bring him their home projects all the time. These are guitars people start building at home and aren't able to get past a certain point and finish. Maybe they can't find the time or have reached a point where their skill level doesn't allow them to continue the build. Kits for building guitars at home are for sale online. Charles likes the challenge and usually makes them play well for the client. Most of the home projects have a successful conclusion.

He recently finished a neck-through fretless bass guitar project that a guy started in his garage. Many people have the energy to start a project, but sometimes they get overwhelmed at the scope of work needed to finish it. Look at me, writing my second book. I never thought of a luthier doing this sort of thing, but it sure makes sense that people would come to him to finish a project they started at home.

Charles worked on a Fender Stratocaster signed by three guys from Pink Floyd. He told me that it was a cool thing to see. He also made a guitar from scratch for Wayne "Animal" Turner of the Hank Williams, Jr. Band. Wayne was the lead guitarist and bandleader on the road, and a session guy for the recordings. Charles has eleven signed certificates of authenticity to put on guitars that he has been commissioned to build for Wayne. These guitars will be based on the first model he made for him. They are shaped like Fender Telecasters, and Charles is using canary wood, which he says is rare and hard to find. He was unable to find any for years, so when he did find a supply, he bought all of it and started shaping bodies for eleven custom guitars. There was more to this story, but since it is all about electric instruments, I will skip ahead to our next point of discussion about Solo Acoustic Musicians.

After thousands and thousands of guitars have come across his workbench, Charles has developed ways to occupy his mind while he is working. He's not operating on autopilot, but I know what he means about having a certain amount of repetition in his job. So he uses his phone to listen to YouTube videos on different topics, or comedy, music, or even scientific lectures. It's something to occupy the part of his mind that is wandering while he is doing the repetitive stuff. I often listen to instrumental music on a YouTube channel through my TV while I type. It helps me relax and focus, and it does not distract me with songs or other people's voices.

As our conversation was winding down, Charles surprised me with one last tip that I had overlooked completely. It's a good idea to stretch your strings after restringing your guitar. After putting on new strings, do you find that they keep going out of tune for a few days? I used to deal with that, too, and then I learned to stretch them out when putting on a new pack. He says that people who play guitar often dread changing their strings because of this issue. But if you stretch your strings out, then you will not go out of tune all the time until your strings are getting old.

He told me his technique for stretching out guitar strings, and I shared one that I made up all on my own. There are several ways to stretch out strings, so I suggest that you search online and find a method that works for you.

If you put them on and tune them up, this is when you stretch them. They will all go flat, so you tune them again and stretch them again. They will go flat repeatedly until they don't. Honestly, this process takes me less than ten minutes. But it saves me the hassle of going out of tune in the middle of songs. Especially throughout the next few nights at gigs. It is not a fail-safe, and your guitar can and will go out of tune for a multitude of reasons along the way. This technique is just a great starting point to avoid the frustration of going out of tune while you are playing.

Other people call it "breaking in the strings." I prefer to do that right away in private instead of on stage in front of an audience. String stretching gives you a lot of tuning stability right away, and you don't have to wait for it to happen over time. This should become part of your standard procedure when replacing a complete set or a single string. It is part of my process every time I change my strings, and I have been doing it for more than twenty years, yet I didn't think to write about it. Thank Charles for bringing it up at the end of our talk. It's not an advanced move, in my opinion, but I did over-look its importance to a working Solo Acoustic Musician or any guitar player.

When we parted ways, I had an hour-long drive home through lightning storms, and I was itching to type up all the advice he had shared with me. The time I spent with Charles was well worth driving through that crazy storm. He shared great advice and tips that may seem like common sense, but can be overlooked or forgotten along the way. Not putting your guitar on a wall hanger that gets direct sunlight is a gem. Stretching your strings is part of my habit, and I didn't think of it until he brought it up. The idea that knowing how to make a simple neck adjustment to an acoustic guitar should be part of every SAM's skill set is also enlightening.

This man can build a guitar from scratch and fix any problem it might have. A good luthier can be hard to find, and they are worth every penny they charge if you want your guitar fixed properly. It was a delight to sit and talk with him. He has a good sense of humor and knows his technical stuff about guitars. I am thankful to call Charles a friend, and I hope as a Solo Acoustic Musician that you can establish a good relationship with a trustworthy luthier near you.

As of today, you can find Charles on social media by looking for the Scroggins Guitar Custom Shop. You might be able to catch him live or watch a video of him working on guitars.

TYPES OF VENUES & GIGS FOR A SAM

Throughout all my years of playing gigs, I had a strict definition of the word venue, but I have relaxed that perspective somewhat. I was always very firm about only applying the word to places with specific criteria. Things like a stage, a house sound system or P.A., a soundman, ticket sales, etc., were what I believed made a place a venue. A civic center, a concert hall, an amphitheater, etc., were venues, but the bars and restaurants I was playing were not "venues" in the strict sense. I have changed my mind about the use of the word and the qualifications for its use.

A Solo Acoustic Musician is a versatile performer and can play gigs in many types of venues. Here is a list and descriptions of the types of venues that I have played. In over thirty years of being a SAM, I have played in many environments and situations. I would like to know if I have missed any, or if you have played in a different type of venue, so that I can add it to the list.

RESTAURANT

Many restaurants that I have played music in were already booking music, and I made my sales pitch or gave my information to the manager in charge of booking. You can reference the booking chapter in SAM1 for more details about booking a gig. It is a numbers game sometimes. So talk with managers and owners at many types of places, because the more venues you call, the more gigs you can get.

There are different types of restaurants, and you can always ask any of them if they would like to try live music. I have made my sales pitch to diners, upscale steakhouses, and other restaurants that didn't typically offer music in the past, and I have booked gigs with some of them. Even if that type of restaurant doesn't traditionally have live music, you might get lucky and find a new place to play.

Just to give you some perspective: When approaching corporate-backed franchise restaurants, remember that they are probably locally owned but follow a corporate structure. They are allowed to hire musicians, karaoke hosts, and DJs or trivia hosts. It's up to the management and local owners if they want to spend money on entertainment. So even if they don't have live music, you can approach them and inquire about being hired. Give it a shot.

I know towns with a vibrant downtown area full of restaurants and bars; I could list examples of cities like this, with more than twenty establishments. In many places, almost all of them have live music, and they can even offer music on more than one night of the week. These areas create multiple opportunities for a Solo Acoustic Musician to find work.

SPORTS BAR

A sports bar is another type of restaurant, but as you might guess, it focuses on a sports theme. Some of these bars will have live music, but be aware that they may cancel you for a major sporting event. In my area of Tampa

Bay, we have a consistent playoff-level pro hockey team called the Lightning. When the playoffs happen, the bar cannot predict the schedule, because if the team wins or loses a game, the schedule will change moving forward. You may or may not be canceled on a night-by-night basis. It's always good to be proactive and look this information up, instead of waiting for the manager of a given restaurant to contact you. They are so busy preparing for the event that they will likely overlook the musician. You can be aggressive and try to salvage your gig by playing before the game, or just rescheduling your date with them. This tactic doesn't always work, but it's worth a try if the gig is valuable enough to you.

PIZZA JOINT

I have played live music in quite a few pizza restaurants, and some of them even had a stage for the performers. These establishments were almost always local mom-and-pop-owned restaurants and not part of corporate chains. Of course, I worked out a deal for free pizza as part of my pay. In my opinion, pizza joints, as I like to call them, can be a mix of sports bar and Italian themes. I have traditionally had fun playing in these places, and as a SAM, I was received well there.

Pro Tip: *Ask the venue if they would like you to supply music on your breaks or if they will want to turn on the house system for break music.*

SEAFOOD RESTAURANT

I grew up at the beach, and there were many seafood restaurants around. Quite a few had live music, and some of my first gigs were in these places. I have spent most of my life near the water, and seafood restaurants are a prevalent theme for me. Many of them have an indoor/outdoor atmosphere and usually incorporate the use of a deck or porch area because they are on or near the water. I enjoy playing in places like this.

I have songs in my songbook covering many genres and styles. I like to play songs about fishing and drinking beer, which usually goes over very well in a seafood restaurant or bar. I enjoy mixing these songs into my sets throughout the night when I play at this kind of restaurant.

SUSHI RESTAURANT

A sushi restaurant wasn't the traditional type of place that hired solo acoustic musicians when and where I grew up. I have played several of these in the last few years, though. They are an absolute joy in which to perform, and something seems to click. I play at a dedicated sushi restaurant and at restaurants with sushi bars. One of the sushi chefs I know is looking at opening a new restaurant and recently asked me if I would play music there when he opens.

IRISH RESTAURANT OR PUB

Another popular type of restaurant that may have live solo acoustic acts is the Irish pub. I have been fortunate to play a few truly authentic Irish pubs with stages for the musicians.

Of the "real" Irish-style pubs that I have been lucky enough to visit, I have found that they try to focus on traditional Irish music. I don't play any traditional Irish songs, so I don't get to play at some places. I admire them for having a direction or theme for their music and sticking to it. I also enjoy going to these places for the music. It's different, and it's authentic. If you want to learn traditional Irish songs, you can get gigs in these bars, and it's a specialized niche worth more than just a St. Patrick's Day gig.

Unfortunately, though, most of the Irish bars in the US are sports bars with an Irish theme. I hate to admit that, but it has been my experience. These bars usually incorporate live music into their schedule. I currently play at a couple of these places, but only from time to time. Cancellations for significant sporting events can happen, as I said in the Sports Bar section, so be prepared to adjust your schedule.

STEAKHOUSE

There are several types of steakhouses, and I have played some of the corporate chains as well as local, individually owned establishments. Some steakhouses are a more casual experience with a country music-style vibe to them, and others can offer an upscale, fine dining type of experience. Like so many of the other venues listed here, the steakhouse can be a very versatile and unique experience — every one is different.

UPSCALE RESTAURANT (REQUIRING RESERVATIONS)

Playing places in this category might require a wardrobe adjustment from the regular gigs that I play. Dressing the part and changing for a particular gig is part of the job as a SAM. In a case like this, I might need to wear dress shoes, khakis, and a dress shirt. It doesn't always have to include a suit jacket, but sometimes I like to step it up and go all out for the gig. You can reference the wardrobe section in SAM1 for more information on this topic. Just remember that for this type of venue, you might want to "dress to impress!"

I also must be very aware of my volume level, and keep things softer than I would at a rocking dive bar. These gigs can still be fun, though, and can pay well. Being a SAM means learning to play effectively at a lower volume. Adapting to different situations and accommodating a variety of clients is especially important to a SAM's ability to stay busy.

I will not be expected to bring my fans, because of the number of reservations. Also, they can be reservation-only and not accept any walk-in customers. I won't be required to promote my show at a venue like this. I often play this kind of place, and I enjoy it immensely. I usually make terrific tips. I also get to take home a meal as part of my pay, and they tend to have fantastic food.

GOLF COURSE/COUNTRY CLUB

A restaurant at a golf course or country club will usually have a golf theme, with some emphasis on other sports as well. I will make a wardrobe suggestion for this type of venue. It might not be necessary to do this, but you can fit in well if you wear a golf shirt, which is a polo shirt with a collar. Most golf course restaurants like to have a somewhat upscale feel, and wearing a shirt with a collar is more appropriate than just a T-shirt.

I played at a golf course restaurant every Sunday afternoon for a year, and I built up a small collection of polo shirts. I found a clearance rack at a department store and over time I bought about ten. I wanted to have a selection from which to choose. While I don't play there anymore, or at any golf course restaurant very often, I am prepared for the situation. I can also use these shirts for the other fine dining restaurants or private parties that I play. These shirts are considered "dressy" and are acceptable to wear loose, not tucked in, which I love. Being comfortable and yet dressed appropriately for a gig is a fine line to balance sometimes.

YACHT CLUB

These establishments have nautical themes and are on the water, and the majority of people in the audience will be club members. Some of them will bring guests. There is a certain exclusivity to these venues because of the expensive membership fees. There are perks to playing at these venues. I don't have to promote my shows, or get people to come, because of the members-only policy. I like playing music by the water and seeing the boats. It's usually in the upper pay range, I'll get good tips, and they'll be serving high-quality food. I like playing at the tiki bar, but I don't like playing in the formal dining room. The yacht clubs I have played at usually have an indoor-outdoor tiki bar near the docks and boats, so for that I will dress in shorts and a polo shirt. This is in line with the wardrobe choices I make for a golf course or country club gig.

Pro Tip: *Pack up your tip can last. You might get a last-second tip while packing up the rest of your gear.*

HOTEL BAR

These venues come in various themes, and you can find them at different hotels. Quite often, you will have a built-in audience who are travelers. They will want to relax, have fun, and spend money. Whether at the beach, in the mountains, or in the city, a hotel bar can be a fun place to play. You can find them everywhere. They can be by a tourist destination, by an airport, in a downtown area, or just anywhere along the highway. I have even mapped out and booked small tours up and down the East Coast and used these types of gigs to get a hotel room as part of my pay. It can be an excellent way to travel if you can work it out. You will be paid for your performance, fed a meal after you are done, and provided with accommodations for the night. A hotel bar gig can also be a good anchor point gig on a road trip. Don't forget to check your local hotels for a bar or restaurant to book yourself a gig.

DIVE BAR

There are a lot of these everywhere. They usually don't have food or much more than snacks. So it's kind of like a taphouse, but with a full range of liquor. I would think of it as having a jeans-and-black T-shirt type of vibe. There is nothing fancy about it; it's a no-frills environment, and a distinct smell always seems to be there. It's usually a mix of spilled booze and cleaner. I think these places are generally neighborhood hangouts, and although they can be a little rough around the edges, they are perfectly safe places to play music. I'm used to the small corner stages that I usually find in a dive bar.

TIKI BAR

This is another versatile style of bar. It can have thatched roofs and umbrellas in the drinks, or just be a bar on the water. The overall theme usually involves the beach and water. Whether it's fishing, surfing, or boating, a tiki bar will predominantly be about some theme within the realm of water. These bars can also be influenced by tropical places, like Key West or Hawaii. The food and drink menus will reflect these influences. You can expect rumrunners and margaritas with fruit and colorful umbrellas.

You can find a tiki-style bar in the mountains, or in a hotel in the desert. The tiki atmosphere is meant to transport you to a tropical vacation vibe no matter where you are. I enjoy playing these bars, and I select songs fit for a beach party and a fun time when I'm there.

BREWERY OR TAP HOUSE

This type of venue has exploded in the last several years. Across the country, thousands of them have opened. Something about combining the crafting of original beer and the crafting of original songs seems to work. You can always play cover songs just like any other gig you do, but I have found that the brewery environment fosters a creative attitude, and some may even prefer original music. If you are looking for a paying gig for your original music, I suggest you approach your local brewery with your sales pitch.

A tap house is a bar that sells craft beers from multiple breweries, with a similar vibe to a brewery. They will likely also offer a wine menu. These are spots for genuine beer lovers, and I think they provide a neighborhood bar atmosphere with a choice of many favorite beers from breweries all around the country. They also offer a brewery-style experience that can be hard to find if you don't live near a brewery. People will congregate here to talk about beer and drink beer together. I always throw in songs about drinking beer when I play these venues.

The majority of these places do not have kitchens or food on-site, so they will often team up with food trucks. I play a few breweries that match up the food truck and the live music schedule simultaneously, and I think it's fun to find out which food truck will be there when I arrive. They often allow food to be brought in or for people to order delivery while at the bar. Although there are exceptions, most of these two types of establishments do not serve hard alcohol liquor drinks.

WINERY OR WINE BAR

A winery gig can be fun, especially after everyone has had some wine. Wineries are usually on large parcels of land where they can grow grapes. Depending on the weather and time of year, you could be playing music outside, surrounded by a beautiful landscape view. I have played wineries with mountain views and fields of grapevines as a backdrop. It's like playing music on a farm, full of happy people relaxing and drinking wine in the countryside.

The inside of a winery's tasting room can be a significant warehouse-type space, and managing your sound and volume is essential. Like a brewery, something feels right about having live music while drinking hand-crafted beverages. I think that there is a subconscious link between the two. It takes time and patience to create wine, and a flair for ingredients to create a blend of flavors for the palate. As musicians, we do this same thing. They are both an art and a skill, and I think they go together nicely.

Wine bars are comparable to tap houses, but instead of beer, the focus is on wine. These bars will have tastings so that you can try wine from different wineries. They can share local, national, and even wines from around the world. Snacks like meat trays or cheese and crackers are most likely available. A monthly wine club meeting is probably on the schedule, and live music will be offered a few nights a week. I have had the pleasure of playing in wine bars across the country, and I think it is an environment that is very receptive to live musicians, especially SAMs.

COFFEE SHOP OR CAFÉ

In my experience, the coffee shop/café venue can be a perfect place to showcase your original songs. Traditionally these places do not have the budgets of other venues and will typically pay less for a guaranteed fee. But the trade-off is that you can play an all-original show and sell your CDs or flash drives. You may also find that you can play here on an off night of the week. You can invite your friends and create an event for yourself. Another bonus is that it can be very much like a listening room in that people will be quieter and listen to you. Most coffee houses are not oversaturated with TVs and the other distractions that you find at bar gigs. This environment can create a wonderful atmosphere to share your original songs with a receptive audience. If you haven't played this type of venue, give it a try. You might be pleasantly surprised by the difference and the result.

DINER/FAMILY RESTAURANT/BRUNCH

Although you can find a brunch gig at other types of restaurants, the main targets for this type of gig would be a diner or a family restaurant. This venue is usually a local breakfast and lunch establishment, and this means they open early in the morning and most likely close around two or three in the afternoon. Some family restaurants will be open for dinner, and occasionally you can find one that will have music in the evening. Don't overlook possible opportunities at your local diner; try your sales pitch on the owner or manager.

CASINO

When I think of a casino music venue, I think of the stage, the lights, and a big band. But as a Solo Acoustic Musician, the reality is likely to be playing in the steakhouse or the tequila bar, which is fine with me. It can be remarkably similar to other gig venues on this list, with some exceptions. Most casinos will have an elevated level of security to go through upon arrival and will also watch everyone's actions, including the musicians. The list of rules regarding conduct will be extensive as well. Where you park your vehicle for load-in, when you take your set breaks, and how you check in to get your vendor lanyard will be explained in detail. I have played music in casinos across the country, and all of them had protocols in place for the entertainers. I even went as far as to print them out and carry them with me in my guitar case. A casino is a very professional, regimented type of venue. Knowing the rules and following them is important.

Not every casino has a hotel attached to it, but many do. This can mean that you can apply the same tactics you use for a hotel bar gig, as far as adding a room to your compensation for the gig. Many casinos will use several different agencies to find and book talent. When you contact and start working with one of them, ask about adding a room to your fee. Hopefully, they can negotiate with the casino on your behalf to get you what you want.

CAMPGROUND/RV PARK

I was surprised years ago when I stumbled onto the fact that there is a little circuit of gigs in campgrounds and RV parks. I have never explored the idea of traveling across the country and gigging at these places, but I think it could make for a good summer tour, especially if you have an RV yourself. I was pleased to find out how friendly everyone was and how excited they were to have a musician come and play for them. A few have even had stages for me to use, and every single one of these venues that I have played made sure that I received a full dinner. It's kind of like a big family reunion, but with strangers. Or maybe another comparison would be that of a barbecue or cookout. A relaxed, comfortable, and fun atmosphere to call a workday, if you ask me.

My suggestion is to call any of these places within an hour from home and offer your services. They may have an on-site restaurant or bar for you to play in, or they might be interested in having you play music out by the pool area. Ask them about their busy seasons or the travel seasons that get the most bookings. This tactic can make it a more accessible sale for you and earn you more fun and tips at the gig.

ASSOCIATIONS OR ORGANIZATIONS

A few examples of what I'm talking about are the VFW, American Legion, Eagles, Elks, Moose, etc. These are usually national or international groups with local clubhouses all over the country and the world. They focus on developing and organizing charity events and fundraisers in their local communities. I have always had fun playing in these places. The people are usually very friendly and receptive to musicians.

These clubs are usually members-only except for specific events. So I would call the club first and not just stop by in person. Once you establish contact with the person in charge of the booking, you can send them information via email or even set up an interview at the clubhouse. I have found that offering an audition set and playing for one hour for free on an off day is a terrific way to get into this type of venue. The reason is that it's a private club of close-knit friends, and the person in charge wants to make sure the musicians that they book will be a good fit. There is a certain amount of responsibility and accountability here that I don't see at some other venues.

SPORTS TEAMS

I live in an area that has pro-level major sports teams. I am also blessed that there are minor league and summer league developmental teams for the pro baseball teams nearby. Because of the warm Florida weather, the pro baseball teams have spring training and summer leagues, here to work on their younger players and get some practice games under their belts. The teams will have events during these seasons, and I get to play music at some of them. If you have access to any level of sports teams, reach out to them and find out who to talk to about events and promotions. You might get a new gig where maybe even a jersey or hat is thrown into the deal.

CITY GOVERNMENT

Cities put on events, festivals, and concerts throughout the year. You can probably find a schedule of events online on the city's chamber of commerce website. There might be a craft festival, a seafood festival, or an event at a local museum coming up soon on the calendar. These events are usually planned far in advance, so shoot for the following year if you don't get on the stage right away. A lot of these events will be annual. You can also call the chamber and find out who you need to talk with for each event listed on their calendar.

As a Solo Acoustic Musician, when I have played these events, I have usually been an opening act before larger bands, or I have played during the breaks between bands. Not all events require full bands, though, and you can find gigs like this pretty easily. Also, besides being an opening act, you could play on a side or smaller stage. Some of these events will have multiple stages for entertainers. Either way, it is excellent for me and usually earlier in the day for a one-hour set. This scheduling means that I typically play another gig that night. These can be awesome gigs to get, so go for it!

Pro Tip: *Keep a pen and a piece of paper in your pocket. Write down your set and break times during your gigs. It's good to have proof of your actions if someone implies that you are taking excessively long breaks. It can be a protective fail-safe for you to have as proof of how you manage your time if a venue manager questions you.*

RETAIL STORES

Have you ever been driving down the street and seen a person dancing while swinging a sign back and forth to promote a business? I think of hiring a SAM to play outside a retail store as an advanced version of the sign dancer person. By playing music, a SAM is drawing attention to the store. People will be able to hear the music across the parking lot or down the street. A passerby may stop to dance or sing along, throw dollars in the tip can, and go into the store to see what they have for sale.

A part of town with several retail stores would probably be the best fit. Anywhere with foot traffic would be ideal. You might even be able to play in a courtyard surrounded by retail shops and convince multiple owners to chip in or to take turns paying you for performances. This idea could also fall under seasonal booking, because they might like spending a little extra money on a musician when it's a busy time of year.

The best times to play would likely be on weekend afternoons. If you already have your weekend nights booked, you might be able to pick up a shift in the afternoon and have a two-gig day.

LIBRARY

Every library has music or an entertainment program with a budget to hire performers. Contact the libraries in your area and see what kinds of things they are doing. You can pitch your show as something new or try to cater a setlist to the themes already in place. If you have various children's songs and like to perform for children, you should definitely call the library. If you can offer an ethnic style of music performance, you might have success highlighting a specific style of music. (See above re: Irish music bars.)

Most libraries are equipped with an extra room for meetings, presentations, conferences, and musical performances. You could find this to be a repeat customer base and be able to book weekday gigs in the mornings, afternoons, or evenings.

RETIREMENT HOMES/ASSISTED LIVING FACILITIES & 55+ ADULT COMMUNITIES

There is an actual circuit for this where I live, because we have an abundance of retirement communities in Florida. I have not played many of these venues personally. I have played in 55+ adult communities, but I have not played in assisted living facilities. I have fun when I do a gig like this, though. I play happy songs, smile, and try not to be too loud. These are usually daytime gigs and can help balance out a calendar if you want to fill in mornings or afternoons.

I have talked about these gigs with other musicians or employees who think that song choices are super important. I tell them that good music is good music. So if I play a song that the audience doesn't know, but I do it well, they will respond accordingly, and so far, I have been right.

BOAT

I have played music on various kinds of boats over the years. Where you live will have a lot to do with finding this gig. Gigs on boats can be affected suddenly by weather changes. Out on the water it can be very windy, and storms can come and go with little warning. I find that the people on the boat are there to have fun, and I like to play upbeat, happy songs for them.

When I lived in Baltimore, I used to play on an old schooner that launched out of the harbor downtown. It was a large boat, probably more of a ship, and held about a hundred passengers (if I remember correctly; it was a long time ago). We would leave the harbor and sail out to Fort McHenry in Chesapeake Bay. The trip would take three hours round trip, and I would play songs while we traveled.

I have enjoyed playing music on yachts for private owners. Like private parties, I usually get offers for this type of gig in person or by referral. There are also yacht and catamaran boat rides that are booked through companies. These charters go on afternoon and sunset tours that launch from the Intercoastal Waterway. Upon leaving the docks, I start to play as we travel into the Gulf of Mexico. Tourists and locals enjoy booking a seat on these charters. There are boats that are big enough to accommodate a band, but most stick with hiring a Solo Acoustic Musician. These gigs are fun, and I have been fortunate to get beautiful weather each time.

I have also been fortunate enough to play some of the larger party boats that launch out of downtown Tampa. In SAM1, I tell a story about a party boat gig in New York City that launched out of Manhattan. These are large boats and can be booked for parties of all sizes or themes and small or large groups of people. It's usually a party atmosphere with a dinner service and a full bar. It is also a gig where I typically need to provide a microphone for an announcement or speech. Some boats do have a house P.A. system with wireless microphones for this situation. So make sure that when you coordinate with the staff upon your arrival, you ask about their needs.

I have never played music on a cruise ship, and I have heard many stories about being a musician on a cruise ship. Some of them were good, and some of them were bad. I have no personal experiences to share with you, but my advice would be to do as much research as you can, and if you choose to try it, sign up for a short-term contract to see if you like it. This way, you will only be gone for a brief time and be able to make an informed decision about what a long-term cruise contract might entail.

LISTENING ROOM

There are different types of listening rooms, but the ones I have had the pleasure of experiencing are ultra-musician-friendly and focused on original music. A stage, house sound, and lights are common in these venues. Ticket sales and the need to promote the show to make money are standard. One major difference between this venue and every other one on this list is the lack of televisions. These kinds of places have a significant focus on music; you can hear a pin drop, everyone in the audience is so quiet when a performer is on stage.

As a Solo Acoustic Musician, this type of venue can be the best possible place to showcase your talents by playing your original music. After playing cover songs in bars and restaurants, you may have developed a fan base or a following. Playing a show of original music on a stage for an hour can be a very special performance. If you can sell out a hundred-seat listening room, you can make good money for one evening of playing your original songs.

You will split ticket sales money with the venue, and the breakdown is usually one of these: 60/40, 70/30, or 80/20.

The performer gets 80%, and the venue gets 20% of every ticket sold. For example, a $10 ticket is $8 for the performer and $2 for the venue. If you sold all one hundred tickets at $10, you would receive $800 for your one-hour performance of your original songs. That is awesome!

As a Solo Acoustic Musician, this is a wonderful outlet and opportunity to share original music. It is a special event and should be treated like one. By only doing this once or twice a year and promoting and selling out the venue, you can maximize your return on the demanding work it takes to create a show like this. You may also see a massive spike in your merchandise sales that night, so make sure you are well stocked up for the event. Recruiting a friend to work your merch table will increase your sales and let you focus on your performance and all the networking with audience members you need to do. Make sure that your merch table is not next to the stage. The venue will probably have a designated spot across the room from the stage and near the entrance or exit doors.

PRIVATE PARTIES AND EVENTS

There are many kinds of private events you can play: birthdays, anniversaries, weddings, holiday parties (Fourth of July, Christmas, New Year's Eve, etc.), graduations, pool parties, barbecues or cookouts, corporate events, neighborhood block parties, and the rare "for no reason at all" excuse to have a private party.

You can wait for someone to ask you to play at their private party, or you can try to create an opportunity for yourself to book one. I think it's fun to call or email local businesses and offer my services to them. Maybe they have a company event coming up, or perhaps I can sell them on the idea of creating an event for their business. Companies can throw parties for the same reasons that private citizens do, like holidays, company anniversaries, or to boost morale and fun. Give it a try. Call or stop into local businesses in your city and talk to someone. Get their email information and make sure you give them your business card. You never know when you might hear from them and get a positive result from your effort.

You can also post on social media that you are available and currently looking to book private events. Who knows when a person might message you about an upcoming party?

This kind of gig can fall in your lap, or you can help create it.

HOUSE CONCERT

Although this kind of venue is someone's private home, it does differ from that of a private party. A house concert is more about the music than a party theme. The focus doesn't have to be on original music, but it is the traditional format. A host will invite a Solo Acoustic Musician to play a show of original music in their home. Then they will invite friends and ask them to bring food and drinks. The number of people is typically limited, to keep the event intimate. Factors like how much room they have in their house and how many people they can accommodate will determine how many people they invite. Typical turnout for a house concert would be between ten to fifty friends. Also, they will ask for or suggest a donation for the musician. This donation is usually between ten and twenty dollars. All the money collected is given to the musician. People gather to share food, drinks, camaraderie and live original music by a SAM.

I have seen different takes on this concept, from a first-time host to a professional host with a stage and sound system. It can be quite a lucrative gig for a SAM. Add up a twenty-dollar donation multiplied by thirty friends, and you get six hundred dollars. A typical original music show is a forty-five to ninety-minute set. So, on average, a one-hour set could make a SAM good money. At the end of the show is the icing on the cake, when the artist can make another windfall of cash by selling merchandise like CDs, stickers, T-shirts, etc. The people who come to this kind of show like to support the artist and can become superfans.

Another thing about this type of venue or show is that if you don't know anyone in your area that is a house concert host, you can ask someone to do it. You can also reach out to people you know in other places and ask them to host a house concert. I know musicians who have made cross-country trips by asking people to host them along the way. It can also include giving the musician a room to stay in for the night. You can visit friends or family, make new fans, and comfortably go on a self-made tour if you do this right.

CHARITY EVENTS (THIS TYPE OF GIG COULD TAKE PLACE IN ANY VENUE)

I always try to donate my time if asked to play a charity event. I touched on this topic in SAM1. When a charity organization or one of its representatives approaches me to play, I will try to help them, if I can do it without losing a paying gig I am already committed to. I do not charge a fee when I decide to play music at a charity event.

CHURCH

Believe it or not, there are paid gigs at churches. They have a budget and can hire Solo Acoustic Musicians to play during services or put on a show. Churches hire SAMs or bands to play concerts for their congregations. Church shows can be any night of the week, and they have people to invite, so the audience is built into the venue. You may have to design your setlist to match your environment. Writing originals or finding proper cover songs are essential for booking a gig at this type of venue.

There is a "circuit" for this type of venue, and it's very competitive. You can book gigs locally or plan a road trip and go on a church show tour. It is not a mainstream or conventional venue for a working SAM to think of calling. But it is a resource, and there are many of them to talk to about bookings. Think creatively, and you might be surprised by the results.

BOWLING ALLEY OR POOL HALL

Bowling alleys might have a lounge that serves food and beverages, and you can find gigs in places like this. It's a family restaurant type of atmosphere inside of a bowling alley. I have only ever played in one of these establishments that had a small stage for musicians; most don't. Most bowling alley lounge gigs are just like other bar gigs, and you are usually separated from the actual bowling.

Some pool halls do have live music, mostly ones that also have a bar. Mind you, this is not a bar with a pool table, this is a large open room with many pool tables that also has a bar.

There is a difference. One in my neighborhood has bands on the weekends and SAMs occasionally on weeknights.

KAVA LOUNGE

While I have driven by a few of these venues in my travels, and I have seen musicians post about playing music at them, I didn't know what they were until I interviewed Chase Harvey, and this is what he told me. I give him credit for this information.

He says they tend to be like a coffee shop/remote workplace during the day. At night, though, it tends to be a mellow hippie vibe for people who don't want to drink alcohol but also want to socialize. He says that he will go to one after a bar gig to have a change of pace and relax. He can grab a coffee and hang out. He told me that Kava is a leaf used to make a tea-like drink. Its origin is in the Pacific islands. It can give you a euphoric vibe.

For him, as with most SAMs, it's a venue that provides a non-alcoholic place to hang out and enjoy music. When he does play at a Kava lounge, he enjoys a different age group and experience with his musical approach. Using his loop pedal and drum pad, he can play instrumental music and express himself differently from the music he plays at the traditional SAM venues. For him, it has become a new outlet for his music that is fun.

BUSKING

Busking is playing in the street or another public place for donations. This is not a type of gig that I have ever played. The busking or street performance "venue" is not a place with an owner; it's usually a designated area where the city or county allows playing music or performing for tips. If you are interested in playing this kind of gig, I suggest you call or visit a chamber of commerce and inquire about where and when you would be allowed to perform. For example, New York has a program called Music Under New York where musicians get permits to play in the subway. Some cities require that you provide identification to obtain a permit. Make sure you stick to their guidelines for when and where you can play your music. If you do not, you can receive a ticket for breaking the rules.

I grew up in Ocean City, Maryland, and there were two designated spots on the boardwalk to busk. If you were playing a guitar with an open case or a tip can in front of you, and you weren't in the right spot, you would get a ticket unless you had a permit. Performers were able to obtain a permit from City Hall for free with a driver's license or other form of ID. The permit would only be valid for one week. It was free, though, so it was easy to renew repeatedly if you wanted to. There is a fishing pier area in Clearwater Beach, near where I live now. They allow face painting, craft/art booths, juggling, etc., and musical performers can busk for tips. You must register with the pier organization through their website or office. Then you will be allowed to perform. I am sure that performers can make a lot of money on a busy night with beautiful weather during the tourist season.

HOMESTEAD, FL TRIP
OCTOBER 31ST —
NOVEMBER 4TH, 2020

After a long summer and a constantly shifting transition from everything being closed to things opening back up, even if partially, I found myself itching for a road trip. I was talking with a friend about going down to southern Florida. The Keys were my most likely destination, but I was also thinking about Marco Island as I had never been there. It had been a while since I got out of the neighborhood, and I felt like I needed an adventure. So, I felt blessed when my friend Jimi, who lives in Miami, called me up with a gig opportunity. Road trip!

I have known Jimi for more than twenty years, but we don't see each other much because we live so far apart. We reached out to each other during the shutdowns through online platforms, and then by phone. It was fun to rekindle an old friendship and reminisce about places and friends from long ago. As we talked, we started to entertain the idea of trading gigs when things got back to normal. Once again, though, months went by before the next time we spoke. That was when he reached out to me with the idea that offered me the adventure for which I had been pining.

Every year in the fall, my friend helps a cause with his musical skills. They raise a substantial amount of money for a local charity. He called me in a last-minute jam to find someone to cover a gig for him. He was scheduled to shoot video footage for the charity all day on a Sunday the following weekend. The gig was in Homestead, Florida, about six hours south of my house.

I did not have a gig that day and quickly decided that I should do it. We started breaking down the details and formulated a plan. The gig would be held at a winery/brewery/restaurant, and that sounded like a fun place.

I had a date, a time, and a place to perform, and I had to figure out the logistics and make a plan.

I would play my Saturday night gig near my home, and when I was done at 10 PM, I would start driving south. I planned to stay at a hotel outside of Naples, FL. It was $100 for the room, and the hotel was at about the halfway point of the drive. The following morning, I would wake up and cruise east across the state on a highway nicknamed Alligator Alley. It's a straight shot through the Everglades.

I made a last-minute change to my plan and decided that instead of taking the big highway, I would go south to Route 41 and drive the old road across the Everglades. After all, I wanted to have an adventure, right? It was a beautiful day, and I saw lots of fan boats coming and going in the water just off the sides of the road. I was driving on the country roads, and there was an authentic old Florida vibe.

I made good time on my drive and arrived on time for the gig. Jimi had already explained where I should park and who I would be meeting. I followed his directions around the complex of buildings and found my way quite easily to where he had told me to be. I went inside and asked for my contact and was directed to the next building. Remember, this was a big place: a winery, a brewery, and a restaurant.

I found my contact, she showed me where to set up, and we talked about what she wanted from me. It was a pleasant conversation, and she introduced me to a bartender who would be able to address any of my needs for food and drinks. Jimi had already filled her in on how far I was driving and what we were doing. She was genuinely nice and very appreciative of me being there. It's always a pleasant surprise when someone goes out of their way to make you comfortable.

I played my music for a very receptive audience and staff. I was hoping to make good tips to help supplement my expenses, and the people did not let me down. Then I tried one of their beers and ordered some food when I was packing up. The manager gave me a check, and I was back on the road. It was almost dark out by this time, and I drove on the main highway to make things easy. It had been a long day, and I was ready to get back to the comfort of the hotel.

I was winging it and didn't have a room booked anywhere. I liked where I had stayed the night before, so I called them and was able to secure the same room. It was on the first floor with a window looking onto the parking lot so that I could see my van easily. It was also at the end of the hall, by the door to the pool deck, which made it easy for me to wheel my cart full of gear to my room. I felt safe there, but I felt even safer with the main equipment in my room. I'm talking about my guitar, pedalboard, and P.A. My mic stand, merch box, and little tables could stay in the van.

I decided to take a slow route home and travel small roads up the west coast of Florida. I didn't have gigs on Monday or Tuesday that week, so I wanted to explore some other towns and avoid the highways as much as possible.

When I left the hotel this time, I headed southwest toward Marco Island and started an adventure home. I found lots of little beach towns and met new people over the next few days. I extended my trip one more night and came home on Wednesday. I would stop anywhere that caught my eye or seemed interesting. I found Delnor-Wiggins Pass State Park, a chill beach to relax on. I grabbed lunch to go from a restaurant right up the street and sat at a picnic table in the shade, looking at the Gulf of Mexico. After a swim and sitting in the sun, I hopped back in my van to continue north.

On this trip, I found new places to call about booking gigs and even met a few of the local musicians who were playing those nights. I found a couple of scenic beach roads on Manasota Key and Casey Key. Both were beautiful. Part of the drive was under a canopy of trees, and immaculate beach houses lined both sides of the road. I even parked at one that was for sale and walked around the side so I could use their beach access for half an hour. I know I was being sneaky, but I was on an adventure and wanted to have a little fun.

I kept inching my way slowly up the road toward home, and eventually the trip was over. I had fun, and I could go on and on about the trip, but I think you get the general idea.

Many of the elements in SAM1 are represented in this story. The opportunity was available through a musician friend, an example of networking. Being on time and managing a travel schedule, crucial to the success of this road trip, was a top priority at the beginning of the story. Transportation was also at the top of the list to make this trip happen.

The gear I brought needed to match the venue's needs. I had to bring both of my Mackie main speakers to accommodate a large indoor/outdoor area. I needed to aim them in different directions. Of course, merchandising was involved during the gig. I had to coordinate with the venue for tax paperwork and promotional materials that included pictures and online links. The load-ins, pre-show, and weather chapters all played a role in the actual gig.

Working the crowd was also a part of the experience. I counted this as a break-even, which is talked about in the booking chapter. I also created new contacts at the venue and can reach out to them to book myself in the future. Remembering to be a pro and act appropriately was also important because I was not only representing myself, but I was also representing a longtime friend and a respected musician.

I was also fulfilled by having an adventure, donating my time and efforts to a worthwhile charity, and enjoying playing music in a new place for many unfamiliar faces. Overall, this story encompasses everything I need to do to succeed as a Solo Acoustic Musician.

 # GATOR COUNTRY

Not long ago, I was playing at a restaurant on a little creek in Hernando County. It's an indoor/outdoor establishment in a small town about an hour north of mine. I feel like I am out in the old Florida country when I am up there.

I was setting up my gear and running cables when I happened to look up and saw an alligator swimming slowly by in the water. Seeing the animal cruising by just validated my feelings. There is a deck railing between me and the water where I can see turtles and fish swimming around. I have played there before, and it's fun to watch the kids throw pellets of feed out onto the water. This was the first time I had seen an alligator in the water, though. It was not a little one, either. I would say it was about eight feet long. At one point, it stopped swimming and lowered itself so that only part of its head was above the water. It stayed still for a little bit, then disappeared under the water.

The gator swam through the tall grass in the water and was gone. It showed up again when I was on a break between my first and second sets, to the children's delight. I was able to get a picture this time, and text friends to show them what was happening at my gig. Times like these reaffirm my decision to avoid a career in an office. Some days at my job, I am blessed to experience added fun.

 **AFTERWORD**

I hope you enjoyed the second book of this series. I intended to offer more information from my own perspective, and interview other full-time working SAMs and share their knowledge with you.

By interviewing other Solo Acoustic Musicians, I tried to find more new advice and real-life stories that apply to being a working SAM. I think I accomplished my goal and learned a few things during the interviews. In SAM1, I only told you stories and advice from my perspective, so it was enlightening for me to listen to and write about the experiences of other Solo Acoustic Musicians. Hearing how other SAMs handle similar situations helps me look at things in a different way. Also, I found it informative to learn new techniques or ways to do things that I wasn't aware of before.

The reason I wanted to interview a luthier wasn't to teach you how to fix your guitar. That would be a book for a luthier to write, and I am sure they are available if you look for one. What I wanted to find out and share with you was tips and advice for a Solo Acoustic Musician, the things that can help you be better at your job and help turn you into a more professional SAM. I chose Charles because I knew it would be fun and that he would tell me, and you, things we should know.

The information in SAM2 is meant to help you reach a new level as a Solo Acoustic Musician. I am always trying to learn something new and get better at every aspect of my job. From the interviews I conducted, I found new insights into the life-style of being a Solo Acoustic Musician. It is a great feeling to know there is a SAM community that shares ideas. Ideas in SAM2, like finding a mentor or being a mentor, are important for our personal growth and those around us. By teaching each other new ideas, we can help each other learn how to be better SAMs.

I feel lucky and blessed by the response I have received for SAM1. I hope you enjoyed SAM2... and be on the lookout for SAM3.

ABOUT THE AUTHOR

Michael Nichols has been a singer-songwriter and working musician for thirty years. He currently lives in the Tampa Bay area of Florida. Growing up singing in a church choir and the school chorus was a great beginning to his life in music. Though he tried several other instruments before putting his hands on a guitar, he didn't get into the drum set, piano, violin, or saxophone. Mr. Nichols started "gigging" for money when he was fourteen years old and has played music in almost every situation possible. After all these years of playing out, he has developed a playbook of the dos and don'ts of being a Solo Acoustic Musician. Michael is still playing almost three hundred gigs a year and staying busy in his community. As a Paul Harris Fellow involved with Rotary International, he has donated money and time to charitable activities over the years. He also intends to share a percentage of proceeds from this book with charitable causes.

 # ACKNOWLEDGEMENTS

I can't say thank you enough to the many people who have decided to purchase *Solo Acoustic Musician: A Practical How-To Guide*. It is truly amazing how many people have emailed or written to me on social media about how the book has helped or influenced them. I am incredibly grateful for the response of strangers all around the world. Cheers to all of you!

You can find links for SAM1 and merchandise on the website

soloacousticmusician.com

Printed in Great Britain
by Amazon

25946041R00128